THE COMPUTER IMAGE

The Computer Image: Applications of Computer Graphics

DONALD GREENBERG

AARON MARCUS

ALLAN H. SCHMIDT

VERNON GORTER

ADDISON-WESLEY PUBLISHING COMPANY

READING, MASSACHUSETTS · MENLO PARK, CALIFORNIA
LONDON · AMSTERDAM · DON MILLS, ONTARIO · SYDNEY

This book was planned, prepared and produced by the Publications Department of Polaroid Corporation.

Director of Public Relations and Communications
SAMUEL YANES

Publications and Exhibitions Director
CONSTANCE SULLIVAN

Project Editor
WILLIAM SAUNDERS

Assistant Editor
ABIGAIL POTTER

Editorial Assistant
NANCY GEERKEN

Production Manager
ALISON GUSTAFSON

Designed by Malcolm Grear Designers, Providence, RI
Printed by Acme Printing Company, Medford, MA

The Computer Image: Applications of Computer Graphics is in the Addison-Wesley Microbooks Popular Series.

Sponsoring Editor
THOMAS A. BELL

Graphics in "Images from the Computer: A Selection," "Computer-Aided Business Graphics," and "Polaroid Instant Photography in the Computer Graphics Camera" were produced on Polaroid films.

Library of Congress Cataloging in Publication Data

Greenberg, Donald.
  The computer image.

  Bibliography: p. 122
  Includes index.
  1. Computer graphics.   I. Marcus, Aaron.   II. Schmidt,
Allan H.   III. Title.
T385.G74   1982   001.55   82-8755
ISBN 0-201-06192-9   AACR2

Table of Contents

An Overview of Computer Graphics

DONALD GREENBERG

What is "computer graphics?" The term is widely used, yet it has a variety of meanings. The computer's ability to draw or to display information certainly falls within the domain of computer graphics. In many engineering industries, documents are automatically drafted using digital plotters to produce high-quality line drawings. Video games and their explosive displays are another application. Much more impressive are the airplane simulation systems currently used for training pilots by dynamically displaying realistic views of the terrain as seen from the cockpit windows. These examples indicate the display capability of today's technology. Not as well known, but perhaps more important, is the ability to draw or scan information into the computer. The information taken in can be two-dimensional, such as pencil sketches for cartoon animations or maps for planning purposes. Or it can be three-dimensional in the form of descriptions of solid objects, such as mechanical parts or automobile bodies. This information, and the method by which it is placed into the computer represents system input, while system output consists of the graphic display produced by the computer. Thus, computer graphics might best be defined as the communication of graphic (non-alphanumeric) data *to* or *from* the machine.

A distinction between *active* and *passive*, or between interactive and non-interactive computer graphics should also be made. Active computer graphics requires two-way communication between the user and the machine. Instantaneous feedback is necessary to provide effective participation between the user and the computer. How would one feel if one tried to draw, and the ink didn't flow from the tip of the pen as it moved, but the line appeared later? For *interactive computer graphics*, the response must be immediate. When commands are invoked to position elements or to rotate objects, the displays must be generated fast enough to give the appearance of active user control. In contrast, the mechanical plotting of a drawing is an example of *passive* graphics and can occur any time after the information has been input. This operation is frequently performed at locations different from the user site, and at periods of low demand, such as night time hours.

Obviously, the requirements of interactive computer graphics systems are considerably different than those of passive graphics operations. The fast response and dynamic displays place enormous demands on the computer system in terms of processing power, storage, and data transmission, but interactive graphics systems are able to display not only the graphical representation of the object being modeled, but possibly the results of analytical routines as well. This important feature allows the designer to participate in an interactive design loop, inserting human creativity into the decision-making process, and constitutes the fundamental characteristic of effective *computer-aided design* systems.

For an effective dialogue to occur between the human and the machine, the communication media must be fast, comprehensive, and comfortable to use. Computer graphics provides this communication language. It is much easier to understand a picture than a verbal or numerical description of the same information. We live in a visual world. We take in most of our information through our eyes. The amount of information obtained visually far surpasses the amounts obtained by our other senses. In computer jargon, "A picture is worth 1024 words."

The use of computers to draw pictures is not new. Digital plotters and point-plotting displays existed thirty years ago. Solutions to differential equations were being displayed at MIT's Lincoln Laboratory on a cathode ray oscilloscope in the early 1950's. The SAGE air traffic control system was used to detect and display the location of aircraft over the continental United States in 1953. The impetus for interactive computer graphics can be traced to Ivan Sutherland's SKETCHPAD system, developed at MIT in 1962.[1] Subsequently, several industries, particularly the aerospace, automotive, and shipbuilding industries, began to develop and use interactive computer graphics as part of their computer-aided design systems. Significant advances, particularly in interactive software, emanated from these efforts. Early entries into this field included IBM, General Motors, Lockheed, McDonnell Douglas, and General Electric. More recently, rapid advances have occurred in the development of algorithms for graphic display. Researchers at the Universities of Utah, Ohio State, North Carolina, Rochester, Cornell, and Rensselaer Polytechnic Institute have all contributed to this knowledge expansion.

Computer graphics is certainly becoming more popular. No recent breakthrough or scientific discovery has made this possible; it is simply that computing and the production of electronic components have become so economical that one can no longer afford to ignore graphics technology. Applications are not restricted to high technology areas, or even to university-level research; the prime usage is likely to be business applications and teaching in elementary schools.

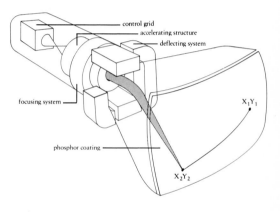

1

Vector or calligraphic display showing a line being drawn on the face of a tube.

1 I. E. Sutherland. *SKETCHPAD: A Man-Machine Graphical Communication System*. Cambridge, MA: MIT Lincoln Laboratory Technical Report #256, May 1965.

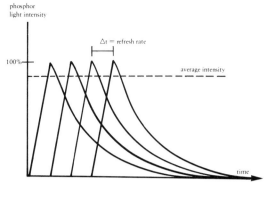

phosphor
light intensity

Δt = refresh rate

100%

average intensity

time

2

Plot of intensity versus time for a vector refresh
display.

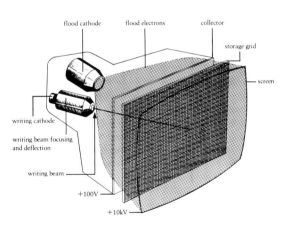

flood cathode   flood electrons   collector

storage grid

screen

writing cathode

writing beam focusing
and deflection

writing beam

+100V

+10kV

3

General arrangement of a direct view storage tube.

This article attempts to provide brief overviews of existing computer graphics technology and of the logical processes required to create a computer-generated image. Various types of display hardware are discussed, and the software logic required to create computer images is described. Techniques for graphical input are also explained. The fundamentals of perspective transformations and the procedures required to generate color displays are then described. Finally, selected applications are presented to demonstrate the diversity, complexity, and the potential of computer graphics.

Computer Graphics Systems

In general, two types of computer display equipment are available: calligraphic or vector displays, and raster video displays.[2] Both types depend on the glow emitted by a phosphorescent screen when bombarded with a stream of electrons.

The vector displays are cathode ray tubes (CRTs) and are unique in their ability to draw from one arbitrary (X_1, Y_1) location on the screen to another (X_2, Y_2) location. Electrostatic or magnetic fields are used to control the movement of the electrons and, thus, the positioning of the beam (Figure 1). If the beam is turned on when it is deflected to various parts of the screen, it leaves a visible trace.

When the electrons strike the phosphor coating, the light given off after the excitation is called *phosphorescence*. The duration of this phosphorescence is called *persistence*, which can last from several microseconds to many seconds depending on the phosphor's characteristics. Normally, the decay is rapid, causing the trace to be only momentarily visible. Thus, in order to produce a steady, flicker-free picture, the same pattern must be *refreshed* frequently (Figure 2). Fortunately, if successive images are drawn fast enough, the human visual response perceives them as a continuous image or series of images. Thus motion can be simulated. Both the movie industry which generates twenty-four frames per second, and the television industry, which generates thirty frames per second, rely on this perception.

An early type of vector display very popular in industry was the direct view storage tube. This device was based on two separate principles. First, a writing beam deposits a positive charge that defines the image on a storage grid mounted directly behind the phosphorescent screen. Second, the image is transferred to the phosphor-coated surface by a flood of low-velocity electrons attracted to the positively charged image (Figure 3). The advantages of these devices are that they are dependable, relatively inexpensive, and can maintain the picture information for long periods. This means that complex images can be drawn and constant refreshing is unnecessary. The disadvantages are their

2 W. M. Newman and R. F. Sproull. *Principles of Interactive Computer Graphics,* Second Edition. New York: McGraw-Hill, 1979.

slow writing speeds and their inability to selectively erase portions of the image. These latter characteristics prevent the simulation of motion except for very simple images.

For truly interactive graphics, fast vector refresh display systems are being increasingly utilized. To produce the flicker-free images, the display must be continually refreshed due to the short persistence of the phosphor. Under computer control, the sophisticated deflection mechanisms available today allow the drawing of many thousands of vectors every thirtieth of a second. Although the image complexity is limited, the rapid generation of images allows the simulation of dynamic motion. However, due to the expense of the deflection mechanisms, this type of display is still relatively costly. Current devices contain specialized hardware that permits dynamic rotations, translations, and perspective transformations. This enables the user to obtain a fully three-dimensional perception of the object being modeled.

To generate a changing sequence of complex displays, the computer has to send large quantities of information to the display device very rapidly. This requires large bandwidth communication channels and much attention from the central processing unit. Initially, the coordinates of each point in each new image were transmitted. Then, buffer memories were added to the display devices, so that while one portion of the buffer was used for refreshing the picture, the other portion was being *updated* with the new image (Figure 4).[3] New systems use intelligent terminals that can store the model description locally and the main computer sends only the information necessary to transform the views. The trend is to place more intelligence at the user station, reducing both the burden on the central computer and the data transmission requirements. In the future, with the advent of more powerful microcomputers, *procedures* for both model creation and display generation will probably be stored locally.

4

Block diagram of a vector refresh display system with a partitioned refresh buffer.

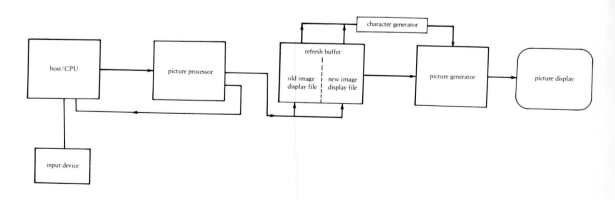

3 *Picture Systems 2 User's Manual.* Salt Lake City: Evans and Sutherland Computer Corporation, 1976.

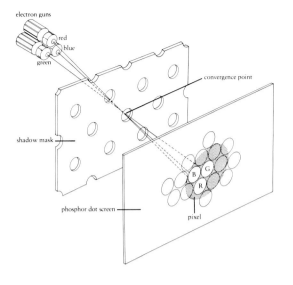

electron guns

red
blue
green

convergence point

shadow mask

phosphor dot screen

B G R

pixel

5a

Shadow mask television tube.

The second category of display devices, raster video displays, consists of two basic components.[4] One component, frequently called a "frame buffer," consists of a fast computer memory large enough to store the image data and able to read the image memory at video rates. The digital output is converted to video output through a digital-to-analog converter (DAC) and is displayed on the second component, a standard or high resolution television monitor. The television monitor contains three electron guns (red, green, and blue), focusing magnets, deflection plates, a shadow mask and a phosphor-coated screen. The phosphor is deposited in a hexagonal dot pattern, resulting in red, green, and blue triads (Figure 5a).

Frame buffers are available in many sizes with various resolutions and levels of intensity. Modern frame buffers use random-access integrated memory circuits to store a rectilinear array of picture elements (pixels). In the digital memory, each pixel has an x,y location and an associated intensity value. Approximately two and two-thirds triads are energized for each pixel location. Thus, like the pictures created by the pointillist painters, each image consists of a matrix of dots. Currently, the most popular frame buffers store a 512 x 512 or 640 x 480 matrix of pixels, although new devices, with 1024 x 1024 resolution, are now available. These latter devices require one million memory locations (Figure 5b).

5b

Color mapped frame buffer system with an overlay plane.

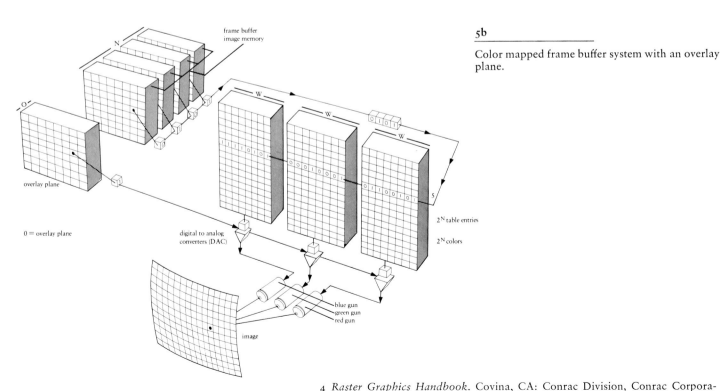

N

frame buffer image memory

O

overlay plane

0 = overlay plane

digital to analog converters (DAC)

W

W

W

S

2^N table entries

2^N colors

blue gun
green gun
red gun

image

4 *Raster Graphics Handbook.* Covina, CA: Conrac Division, Conrac Corporation, 1980.

The intensity of the picture element is a function of memory depth. A black and white image requires only one bit per location. Eight bits will allow 2^8 or 256 different intensity levels. If color maps are used, the user can select 256 colors from a very large range of possibilities. A three-channel, 8 bit/channel display can generate 2^{24} colors simultaneously. To create a picture, it is necessary to write and store the appropriate intensity for each pixel in the image array. The software to perform this operation is discussed below.

Once the image is stored, the information is traced out in *raster* fashion line by line in an ordered and sequential manner. All television systems use this rectilinear scanning system. The beam moves horizontally from left to right, tracing alternate scan lines in $\frac{1}{60}$ second. After vertical retrace, the even-numbered scan lines are displayed in the next $\frac{1}{60}$ second. This *interlacing* allows the picture to be rendered fast enough to prevent flicker. A single *frame* consists of the odd and even lines. A standard 525-line television scanning system is composed of 480 rows and 512 columns.

The major advantage of raster devices is their ability to display halftone and color images as well as vector images. Because of the economy of the television monitors, the decreasing cost of computer memory, and the desire for color images, these devices are rapidly becoming more popular. Their disadvantages are the large amounts of memory required to store the image, the time required to write the image, and the high data transmission rates. Only specialized expensive systems are capable of generating dynamic color images, although, as with the vector devices, the trend is to place more intelligence in the frame buffer, which may allow limited dynamic capability in the future.

In addition to the display hardware, a truly interactive environment requires a graphical input device. The user should be able to "point" to items already displayed on the screen or to "position" new items. The most common graphical input devices are 1) the light pens and 2) the digitizing tablets and their accompanying stylus. The light pen is a passive, photocell device, technically similar to an "electric eye." When the light pen is pointed at the screen of a CRT, a software tracking program in the computer readily identifies the photocell's (light pen's) position. A digitizing tablet is a positional device that determines, either electronically or acoustically, where the stylus is located. One can thus input graphical information to the computer in much the same way as one would create a drawing.

Picture Generation

The process of creating a continuous-tone computer image of a simulated object can be subdivided into five major tasks. First, a mathematical description of the object must be defined and input into the computer. Second, the three-dimensional description must be transformed into a two-dimensional perspective image. Third, a determination of all visible lines or surfaces must be made. Portions of the scene that are out-

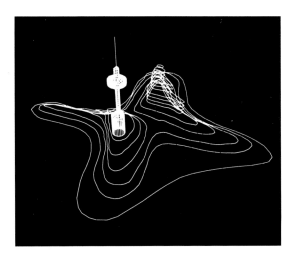

6

Sectional contours used to describe a three-dimensional shape. A television tower on a mountain was described in less than a minute by tracing in the contours at different elevations. (Program *Wire* by Marc Levoy, Program of Computer Graphics, Cornell University.)

side of the cone of vision are removed and lines or surfaces not seen by the observer must be eliminated. This process is called the visible line or visible surface algorithm. Fourth, an illumination model determines the color or shade of each surface or part of the environment. Fifth, the appropriate red, green, and blue intensities must be selected to represent the color specified by the shading model. Each of these operations is described in greater detail in the following sections.

Geometric Models

Before discussing the operations for generating an image, we will describe the techniques available for creating a geometric model.

While the ability to generate realistic images has advanced substantially, the art of inputting the geometric descriptions into the computer has not improved as rapidly. The difficulties inherent in communicating spatial or graphical information to the computer have all too frequently frustrated computer graphics users and prevented the creation of an acceptable dialogue between user and machine. Cumbersome or mathematically complex input methods discourage or prohibit the utilization of automated design procedures by non-technically trained people. A viable input system must permit users to easily define an object, manipulate and edit the object description, combine elements, and rapidly display the composite results to provide visual feedback. Truly interactive computer graphics systems require graphical input devices. The most common graphical input devices are the light pen and the digitizing tablets previously described.

A number of geometric modeling systems are now becoming available to perform these operations, although many are not sufficiently interactive.[5] Most systems rely on constructive solid geometry to combine primitive elements into complex object descriptions.

Primitive elements may be defined in three ways: numerically, graphically, or procedurally. All descriptions eventually provide the geometrical and topological information defining the vertices, vertex coordinates, lines, and surfaces.

Typing numerical input through a keyboard is an accurate but cumbersome, time-consuming, and non-interactive approach. Graphical input methods are becoming more widely accepted and consist of many approaches, some of which are discipline-specific. Several of these techniques are described below.

One very popular method is known as "lofting," where a set of serial cross-sections of an object are interactively defined. This is like tracing the contours from a topographic map. Each contour has a precise elevation (Figure 6). The computer can automatically combine these two-dimensional definitions to create three-dimensional shapes. Since all information is input in two dimensions, standard interactive graphical routines such as inking, pointing, and positioning can be used.

5 A. Baer, C. Eastman, and M. Henrion. "A Survey of Geometric Modeling." *Inst. Physical Planning Rep. 66*, Pittsburgh: Carnegie-Mellon University, March 1977.

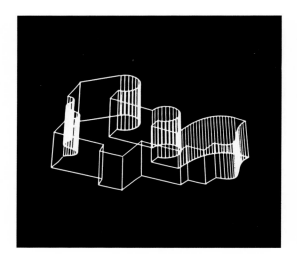

Three-dimensional solid formed by linear extrusion method. (Program *Volume* by Wayne Robertz, Program of Computer Graphics, Cornell University.)

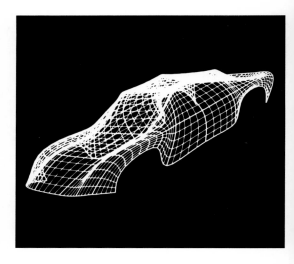

8

Free-form sculpted surface defined by "patches." (Program by Brian Barsky, Program of Computer Graphics, Cornell University.)

The major disadvantage of this technique is the large amount of data required to define amorphous shapes accurately. For this reason, numerical procedures that can accurately represent these three-dimensional surfaces with compressed data have been implemented. Frequently, this is accomplished using parametric curve and surface definitions. This method is often used in cartography or in aircraft or ship design when the cross-sectional profiles are known.

A second approach can be thought of as an extrusion method (Figure 7).[6] A line can be generated from a point, a plane from a line, and a solid from a plane. In each case, the direction of the extension can be controlled and has a unique relationship to the original two-dimensional definition. This "sweep representation method" is very appropriate for the definition of mechanical parts or for architectural design.

Free-form sculpted surfaces are also frequently used, particularly for surfaces curved in two directions, such as the body of an automobile. Although these surfaces can be defined using parametric lofting methods, it is more common to use "patch" definitions. The surface is formed by a mesh of "patches" (Figure 8)[7]. Each "patch" is defined by points or curves in two parametric directions. Thus, any point on the surface is a function of each of the four boundary curves. It is advantageous to use mathematical formulations which allow "local" control, and thus the ability to modify one portion of the surface without affecting other portions.

6 W. Robertz and D. P. Greenberg. "A Graphical Input System for Computer-Aided Architectural Design." *CAD '80 Proceedings 4,* March 1980, pp. 715-723.

7 S. A. Coons. "Surfaces for Computer Aided Design of Space Forms." Cambridge, MA: MIT Project MAC, *Technical Report #41,* June 1967.

Aircraft bulkhead. Complex objects can be described by combining the primitive object definitions into a composite solid. (Department of Computer Science, University of Utah.)

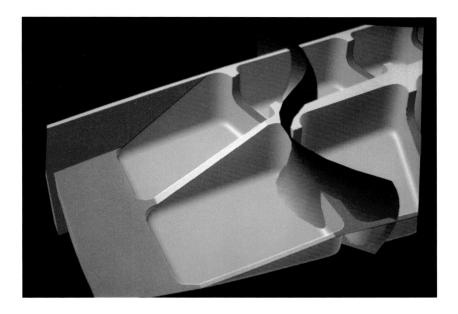

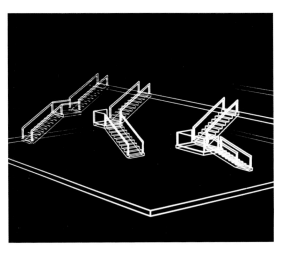

9

Example of "procedural modeling." Single-run, angle-run, and scissor stairs. (Program *Topdrawer* by Eliot Feibush, Program of Computer Graphics, Cornell University.)

One very powerful method, called "procedural modeling," is likely to become very important in the future.[8] In this method, the object geometry is not defined explicitly, but is represented as a "procedure" to which arguments or parametric variables are passed. For example, the stairs generated in Figure 9 required only three input variables: the height, width, and stair type.

No matter how the initial objects are created, a completely general system will allow users to combine these entities to create composite objects. Such computational functions as the Boolean operations of union, intersection, and difference, will allow the hierarchical construction of complex solids. Although research must still be conducted on the geometric intersection of parametrically defined, free-formed surfaces, constructive solid geometry systems for planar polyhedra now exist (Figure 10) and are used in industry.

Perspective Transformations

Once the task of inputting a mathematical description of the object has been completed, the next step is to generate the display. The opportunity to receive immediate visual feedback of what has been defined is one of the major advantages of computer graphics. In any of the input methods discussed previously, each point is located in space by its three coordinates in the object coordinate system. If only line drawing images are desired, the total environment can be described as a set of lines, each with a beginning point and an end point. When solid

8 M. E. Newell. "The Utilization of Procedure Models in Digital Image Synthesis." University of Utah Computer Science Dept., *UTEC-CSc-76-218*, Summer 1975.

Flagellation, circa 1451 (after restoration, 1969). This famous painting by Piero della Francesca illustrates the illusion of depth. The oblique lines, gradation of the tiles, and relative sizes of the figures all contribute to the perspective. (Galleria Nazionale della Marche, Urbino, Italy.)

objects are desired, or where color images are displayed, the objects are normally described by planar polygons, defined by their vertices or bounding lines. Even free-formed surfaces can be triangulated to meet this requirement.

The three-dimensional description of the environment to be displayed must first be transformed into a two-dimensional perspective image. Historically, the laws of perspective geometry were first mastered during the Renaissance (Figure 11).

Today, in mechanical drawing courses, one learns to create perspective drawings by using vanishing points. However, the actual geometric and visual logic for constructing a perspective drawing is to determine the intersections of the view rays emanating from the observer's eyes, with an imaginary picture plane. The view ray is defined as the line connecting a point in the environment with the eye of the observer. The picture plane is an imaginary plane, perpendicular to the line of sight, and a fixed distance from the observer (Figure 12).

To mathematically calculate the position of a point on the display screen that corresponds to a point on some object, the standard procedure is to first transform the point from the *object coordinate system* to the *eye coordinate system*, where the origin is fixed at the viewpoint and the Z_e axis is pointed in the direction of view. The coordinate system is fixed to the observer's eye: it moves and rotates as the eye moves and the head rotates (Figure 13). A viewing transformation matrix is used to enact this transformation. Note that the eye coordinate system is a left-handed Cartesian coordinate system, with the X_e axis to the right and Y_e upward to align with the X_s and Y_s axes of the display screen.

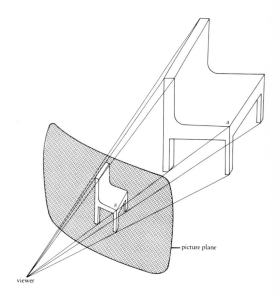

picture plane

viewer

Perspective projection.

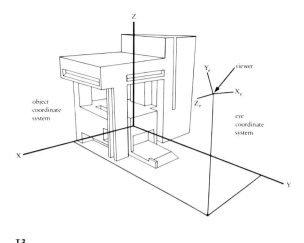

13

Object and eye coordinate systems.

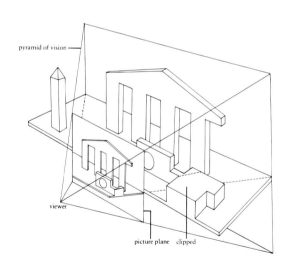

14

Pyramid of vision. Objects outside of the frustum of vision are "clipped" and do not appear on the picture plane.

A perspective display can be generated simply by projecting each point of an object onto the picture plane. The coordinates (X_s, Y_s) of the projected image are easily computed from similar triangles, but require dividing by the depth (Z_e) coordinate value.

After the perspective transformation is completed, points and lines outside the field of vision must be excluded. For undistorted images, the normal cone or pyramid of vision used has an opening angle of approximately 60°. This defines a window on the picture plane. The boundary of this window usually coincides with the edges of the display device, such as the television screen. All portions of the image outside this window must be mathematically "clipped" and removed from the scene (Figure 14).

These operations form the basis for the perspective transformation and can be concatenated into a single matrix multiplication that includes coordinate transformation, clipping, and perspective division. New display devices have now implemented this matrix multiplication in the hardware.

Visible Line/Visible Surface Algorithms

The most difficult and computationally expensive portion of the software procedures is the solution of the visible line or visible surface problem. After the perspective computations, all points in the environment have been transformed. However, the computer does not know which portions of the environment are not visible. Surfaces that are hidden from view, or portions of surfaces that are occluded, must not be displayed. In real life, this problem does not exist since we can not see through opaque objects. For vector displays, it is only necessary to determine the end points of the visible line segments. For raster displays, it is necessary to compute the visibility at each point (pixel) of the image plane. This problem is basically a *sorting* problem for which there are many available solutions.[9] For a polygonally defined environment, each polygon must be compared to every other polygon to determine which one is closest to the observer. The more complex the environment, the greater the number of polygons to be compared and the longer the computation time. A number of ingenious approaches to this problem have been devised. In general, solutions can be categorized as object space or image space algorithms. In object space solutions, the calculations are performed in three dimensions and at the precision of the computer. Image space methods retain the depth information (z) but sort by lateral position of the picture (x, y) and only to the resolution of the display device.

After the perspective transformation and clipping operations have been completed, a large number of polygons from the original polygonally defined environment still remain. If the component of the poly-

9 I. Sutherland, R. Sproull, and R. Schumacker. "A Characterization of Ten Hidden Surface Algorithms." *ACM Computing Surveys 6,* March 1974, pp. 1-55.

gon normal in the z direction is the same as the view direction, the polygon is "back-facing" and can not be seen from the observer's position (Figure 15). The removal of these back-facing polygons from the scene is known as "culling."

At this stage, it is still necessary to sort the remaining front-facing polygons in the scene to create the final image. In order to reduce the computational expense, all standard algorithms utilize some form of "coherence." The term "coherence" is used to describe the extent to which the environment or the picture of it is locally constant.

Three prevalent image space methods are "windowing," "scan line," and "depth buffer" algorithms. Windowing algorithms recursively divide the image into smaller windows until either the visible contents of the window are simple enough to determine, or the window is as small as the desired resolution of the picture.[10] Thus, the subdivision occurs only where necessary and the computation time is roughly proportional to the visible complexity of the image (Figure 16). This method is an example of the use of the area-coherence of the image.

Scan line algorithms sort only those planes in object space that are intersected by a plane containing the given scan line (Figure 17).[11] Since a raster television display generates its image by sweeping horizontally across alternate scan lines from top to bottom, the information from the algorithm is already ordered for the display. The fact that the succeeding television scan line is likely to be similar to the previous one provides additional information called "scan line coherence," which can further improve the efficiency of the computations. Special purpose computer hardware using this approach can perform the calculations fast enough to simulate motion. In contrast, when the computations are executed in software, the execution time may reach several minutes for complex images.

The depth buffer algorithm is the simplest of all hidden surface algorithms and is a brute force approach. Its objective is to independently calculate the intensity of each pixel for the hidden surface display. This intensity will be based on the color of the polygon closest to the observer for that particular pixel. Because the perspective display of the object is an orthographic projection of the distorted object, the depth calculation is greatly simplified. For each pixel (x, y) the value of z can be obtained by solving each polygon's plane equation. The depth and color of the closest polygon is stored in a depth buffer and an intensity buffer. Storage requirements are large and depend on image resolution, and performance is related to image complexity. However, because of its simplicity, the algorithm lends itself to hardware implementation.

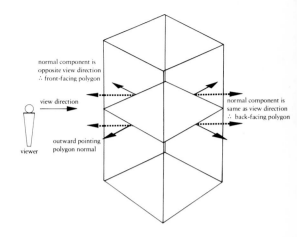

15

Culling. Visible surfaces of a three-dimensional object must be established for the computer if it is to "paint" a realistic picture on the television screen.

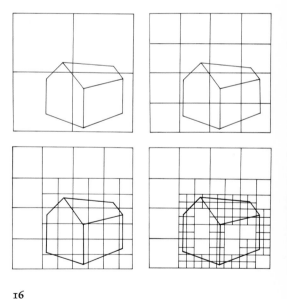

16

Warnock's windowing algorithm. If the information within a window is too complex to decipher, the square is subdivided. Once the contents are known, the display within the square can be shaded.

10 J. Warnock. "A Hidden Surface Algorithm for Computer Generated Halftone Pictures." *C. S. Tech. Report 4-15*, University of Utah, June 1969.

11 G. S. Watkins, "A Real-Time Visible Surface Algorithm." Ph.D. Dissertation, University of Utah, 1970.

There are two disadvantages to these image space algorithms. First, information is lost because of the sampling nature of the algorithms, which calculate intensities only at discrete sample points. This "aliasing" frequently reveals itself in the jagged edges that bound the displayed polygons or in the loss of small polygons that are not sampled. Second, although the image space algorithms do determine the intensities required for a single static image, they ignore much of the environmental information, which could be used for shadowing, texturing, or anti-aliasing. Most object space algorithms avoid these problems by maintaining the full three-dimensional environmental data and carrying out the computations to machine precision.

One particularly useful object space algorithm returns visible polygons or portions thereof as polygonal output data.[12] The visible polygons are obtained by pairwise polygon clipping, such that the shapes of shallower polygons are clipped from those further away from the viewer. The polygonal output from this "cookie-cutter" approach is useful in a variety of ways. The resulting output can be used for both raster and vector displays, since it can yield both visible lines and visible surfaces. More importantly, the polygonal form of output can be used to eliminate aliasing problems and to improve the efficiency of texture and shadow algorithms. Although computationally expensive, improvements that are dependent on image complexity will probably make these algorithms more useful.[13]

Shading Models

Once the visible surfaces have been determined, it is necessary to compute the correct intensity values for each pixel in the shaded images. This requires an accurate model of how objects reflect light. Accurate reflectance models must describe both the color and the spatial distribution of the reflected light. For most shading algorithms, the intensity values used to simulate the reflected light are a function of the light source composition and direction, the surface orientation, and the surface properties. A variety of illumination and reflection models exist, and are used to create realistic images of curved surfaces, even if they are polygonally defined.

When light strikes a medium, three things can happen. First, the light can be *transmitted* through the medium and out the other side, such as with transparent or translucent objects. Second, the light can be *absorbed* by the medium and transformed into heat. Third, the light can be *reflected* from the surface.

The most common shading models treat reflected light as consisting of three components: *ambient, diffuse,* and *specular.* The ambient

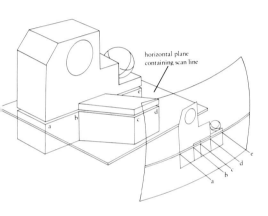

17

Watkin's scan line algorithm. (a) Polygons in object space, which are intersected by the horizontal plane containing the scan line must be sorted, establishing (b) the color segments that should appear on the scan line of the TV display.

12 K. Weiler and P. Atherton. "Hidden Surface Removal Using Polygon Area Sorting." *Computer Graphics II,* Summer 1977, pp. 214-222.

13 S. Sechrest and D. P. Greenberg. "A Visible Polygon Reconstruction Algorithm." *Computer Graphics 15,* August 1981, pp. 17-27.

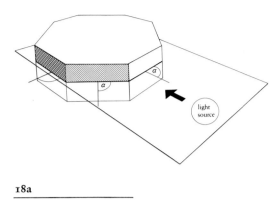

18a

Diffuse reflection—Lambert's Law.

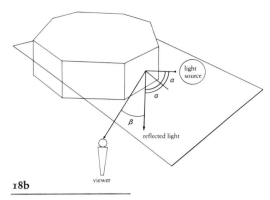

18b

Specular reflection from a smooth surface.

component represents light that is assumed to be uniformly incident from the environment and reflected equally in all directions by the surface. The diffuse and specular components are associated with light from specific light sources.

The diffuse component represents light that is scattered equally in all directions. The simplest illumination model is based on Lambert's Law for the reflection of light from a perfect diffuser. Lambert's Law states that "the intensity of light leaving a surface is proportional to the cosine of the angle between the light vector and a normal vector perpendicular to the surface" (Figure 18a).

The implication is that the reflected light is scattered equally in all directions. Thus, the viewer's position with respect to the surface orientation does not affect the intensity. It is frequently assumed that some portion of the diffuse reflection can be attributed to ambient lighting, and modeled as a constant term. This prevents surfaces that do not receive light directly from a source from being rendered completely black.

Specularly reflected light reflects directly off the surface of an object without entering it. Such reflections occur when light reflects off a mirror. The angle of incidence is the angle between the light ray hitting the surface and the normal vector to the surface. The angle of reflection equals the angle of incidence. Since such a ray reflects off the surface only at a specific angle, it can be seen by the observer only if the eye is located at a specific place (Figure 18b). This implies that the amount of specularly reflected light an observer can see depends, not only on the direction of the light vector and the surface normal vector, but also upon the sight vector, that is, the line that indicates in what direction the observer is looking. How much of the light the eye can see is dependent on the angle between the reflection vector and the light vector,

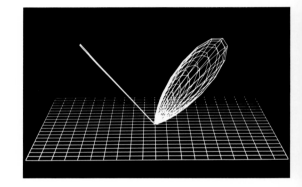

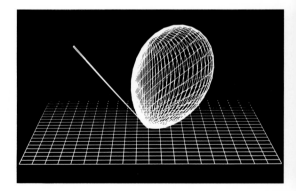

19a,b

Specular reflection from a rough surface. (Rob Cook, Program of Computer Graphics, Cornell University.)

Effect of diffuse and specular model coefficient variations. The spheres were rendered by use of the approximate reflection model. As the value of the specular exponent is increased, the surface appears glossier. (Roy Hall, Program of Computer Graphics, Cornell University, 1981.)

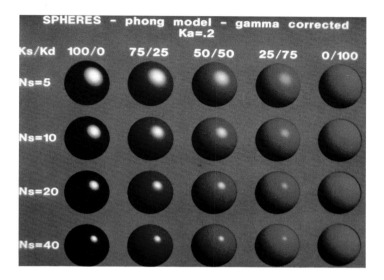

and the spatial distribution of the reflected light. For smooth surfaces, the specularly reflected light is focused along the reflection direction. For rough surfaces, the reflected light is more spread out (Figure 19a, b). This effect can be approximated mathematically. The results obtained by varying the parameters controlling the diffuse and specular terms are shown in Figure 20.

This approximate shading method has been applied to polygonally-represented environments. Gouraud linearly interpolated the diffuse intensity values in scan-line order across the face of a polygon to create the illusion of a diffusely shaded smooth surface.[14] Phong improved on this method by interpolating the surface normals to calculate both the diffuse and specular highlights.[15]

Recently, more realistic illumination models have been published by Blinn and Cook.[16, 17] These models accurately account for the directional distribution of the reflected light on a wavelength basis as a function of surface roughness and slope, the material's properties, and the reflection geometry. This angular spread of the specular component is based on the assumption that the surface consists of microfacets, each of which reflects specularly. Only facets whose normal orientation is in the mirror direction contribute to the specular component of reflection. A facet slope distribution function represents those facets oriented in the mirror direction.

14 H. Gouraud. "Computer Display of Curved Surfaces." Ph.D. Dissertation, University of Utah, 1971.

15 B. T. Phong. "Illumination for Computer-generated Images." Ph.D. Dissertation, University of Utah, 1973.

16 J. F. Blinn. "Computer Display of Curved Surfaces." Ph.D. Dissertation, University of Utah, 1978.

17 R. L. Cook and K. E. Torrance. "A Reflectance Model for Computer Graphics." *Computer Graphics 15,* August 1981, pp. 307-316.

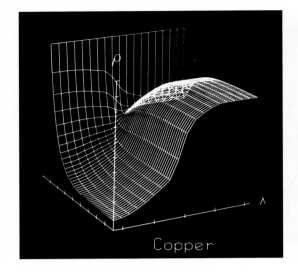

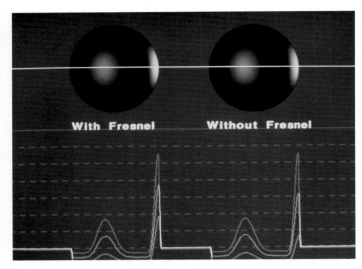

Fresnel diagram of a copper mirror. The reflectance is a function of wavelength and incidence angle. As the incidence angle approaches the grazing angle, the color of the reflected light approaches that of the light source. (Rob Cook, Program of Computer Graphics, Cornell University, 1980.)

22

Fresnel color shift. (Rob Cook, Program of Computer Graphics, Cornell University, 1980.)

The last model accounts for the change in the spectral composition as a function of both wavelength and angle of incidence. As the incidence angle approaches the grazing angle, the color of the reflected light approaches that of the light source (Figure 21). Calculation of the color shift can be computationally expensive, but it accurately represents the true behavior of reflected light. Figure 22 shows two spheres that illustrate the Fresnel effect of the angular variation of the spectral composition. The spheres are lighted, identically, by one light near the observer and by another on the far side of the observer. Graphs at the bottom indicate the red, green, and blue values of every pixel on the scan line and indicate the color shift at near grazing angles.

"Ray-tracing" schemes combine the hidden surface algorithm and the shading model.[18] Since the intensity of each pixel in the image must be calculated, a "tree of rays" is extended from the viewer, through each pixel, to the first surface encountered. From there, for each ray, the reflection directions are calculated, and the ray continues to other surfaces and light sources. The global illumination information allows accurate simulations to be created (Figure 23). When transmission and refraction of light are considered, transparent objects can also be modeled (Figure 24).[19]

18 T. Whitted. "An Improved Illumination Model for Shaded Display." *Communications of the ACM 23*, June 1980, pp. 343-349.

19 D. S. Kay and D. P. Greenberg. "Perceptual Color Spaces for Computer Graphics." *Computer Graphics 13*, 1979, pp. 158-164.

23

An image consisting of polygons and curved surface "patches" generated by a "ray-tracing" scheme. (Turner Whitted, Bell Laboratories, 1980.)

24

Transparency simulation. A nonexistent champagne glass, modeled by simulating the reflection, transmission and refraction of light. (Doug Kay, Program of Computer Graphics, Cornell University, 1979.)

Color

Methods for specifying the appropriate variables defining color for computer graphic displays fall into two categories. The first category consists of realistic image generation where the problem is to replicate or simulate an existing or hypothetical environment. The second category involves "pseudo-coloring," where the color is used as an abstraction to symbolically represent some parameter or characteristic value.

Recall that a color television monitor has three electron guns, one for each of the three primaries, red, green, and blue, of the additive color system. The screen is composed of triads of red, green, and blue phosphor dots, and a color is produced by simultaneously exciting each of the three phosphors by controlling the voltages to each of the three electron guns (Figure 5a).

If the phosphor dots are spaced closely enough, and the observer's distance from the screen is large enough, the eye will spatially integrate the three luminances into a single color sensation. For realistic image generation, the problem is to determine the magnitude of the electron gun voltages such that the color sensation produced by the image approximates the color sensation experienced by an observer watching a corresponding scene in the real world.

How can this be accomplished using only three colors? In a very old experiment (Newton, 1730; Grassman, 1853), light from a test lamp shining on a white screen was matched by an observer who could regulate the intensities of each of the three primary colored lights (Figure 25a).

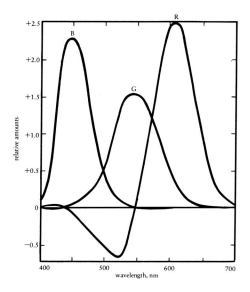

25b

Response matching functions for three primaries: R=700nm, G=546nm, B=436nm.

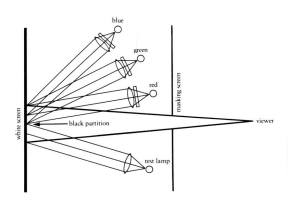

25a

Test arrangement for Grassman's experiments.

This led to the trichromatic generalization theory which states that most colors can be matched by additive mixtures of suitable amounts of three fixed primary colors. The choice of primary colors is limited by the fact that none of the primary colors can be matched with an additive mixture of the other two. Red, green, and blue, which closely correspond to the long, medium, and short wave receptors of the human visual system, are commonly used.

It was found experimentally that all possible test colors could not be matched. For example, a bright yellow could not be matched by any combination of red and green. However, by adding blue to the bright yellow light, a match could be obtained. Thus, if "negative amounts" of light could be used, all of the spectrum lights could be matched. Tests performed for a full set of equal energy spectrum lights indicated the amounts of red, green, and blue primaries needed to match each visible wavelength for the normal observer. These curves, shown in Figure 25b, are known as the "response matching functions."

For any stimulus, it is then possible to create an equivalent color sensation with three primaries by multiplying the spectral energy distribution by the response matching functions on a wavelength by wavelength basis (Figure 25c). The amounts of the three primaries are known as the tristimulus values. A monitor's red, green, and blue phosphors can thus be illuminated in varying proportions to create the same tristimulus values. Although the composite set of spectral energy distributions may not be the same as the original stimulus, the resultant tristimulus values are equal. This is called a "metameric" match.[20]

The goal, then, is to find the proportions of phosphor illumination that produce a spectral energy distribution that is a metamer of the spectral energy distribution of the reflected light of the scene being represented. To produce an equivalent color sensation on a color television monitor, the laws of trichromatic color reproduction[21] are used to convert the spectral energy distribution of the reflected light to the appropriate red, green, and blue values for the particular monitor being used.

If the tristimulus values are known, every color sensation can be uniquely described by its location in a three-dimensional color space. Although the red, green, blue space is most common, for computer graphics the XYZ space is more appropriate. Fortunately, any point in one color space can be linearly transformed to a point in another color space. The XYZ system is convenient because the numerical values are all positive, and the Y values contain all of the luminance information.

A point in this space can be specified with three coordinates, the color's XYZ tristimulus values. Any given spectral energy distribution can be associated with a point in the XYZ color space and thus with its tristimulus values. The red, green, and blue phosphors of a monitor can

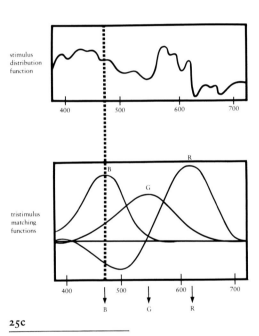

stimulus
distribution
function

tristimulus
matching
functions

25c

Tristimulus Value Calculation.

20 R. W. G. Hunt. *The Reproduction of Color*, Third Edition. England: Fountain Press, 1975.
21 *Ibid.*

be illuminated in varying proportions to produce a set of spectral energy distributions which define a region of XYZ space called the "gamut" of the monitor. The monitor has a maximum luminance at which it can reproduce a given chromaticity. Any XYZ values representing luminances greater than this maximum are outside the gamut of the monitor[22] (Figure 26).

For any color within the monitor's gamut, the gun voltages are determined by calculating the XYZ tristimulus values that are associated with the spectral energy distribution of the reflected light and then calculating the RGB values that produce a spectral energy distribution with the same XYZ tristimulus values. To do this, the spectral energy distribution of the reflected light is multiplied at every wavelength by the equivalent XYZ matching functions. The resulting spectra are then integrated to obtain the XYZ tristimulus values. These XYZ values are converted by a matrix multiplication to RGB linear luminance values for a particular set of phosphors and monitor white point. The linear luminances are then converted to RGB voltages, taking into account the nonlinearities of the monitor and the effects of viewing conditions.

For the selection of "pseudo-colors," several geometric transformations have been proposed for the RGB gamuts of typical color reproduction devices.[23, 24] These provide an excellent terminology for specifying color and are useful in applications where the available gamut is simply seen as a palette of colors.

The use of uniform color spaces can help solve computer graphics pseudo-color selection problems. Uniform color space means that each color in a set is perceptually equidistant from its neighbor. Uniform color spaces are necessary in a display of scalar, vector, or tensor fields, such as stress or temperature levels, on three-dimensional surfaces. This is an important application in engineering design and analysis.

Image Enhancements

Several methods exist to further improve the realism of computer-generated images. The removal of aliasing artifacts or the addition of shadows and textures will improve image quality.

Sampling converts a function into a sequence of discrete values. If the sampling rate is insufficient, either because the sample intervals are too large or the function changes too rapidly, then the discrete values will contain aliasing artifacts.

In computer graphics, this phenomenon appears in raster displays since the image is generated as a sequence of discrete sample points, rather than as a continuous signal. The most common aliasing artifact

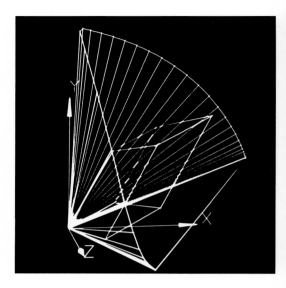

26

Typical color television monitor gamut: the cone of realizable color drawn to arbitrary length in XYZ space. The shape and position of a typical color television monitor gamut is shown within this envelope. (Gary Meyer, Program of Computer Graphics, Cornell University, 1980.)

22 G. W. Meyer and D. P. Greenberg. "Perceptual Color Spaces for Computer Graphics." *Computer Graphics 14*, July 1980, pp. 254-261.

23 G. H. Joblove and D. P. Greenberg. "Color Spaces for Computer Graphics." *Computer Graphics 12*, August 1978, pp. 20-25.

24 A. R. Smith. "Color Gamut Transform Pairs." *Computer Graphics 12*, August 1978, pp. 12-19.

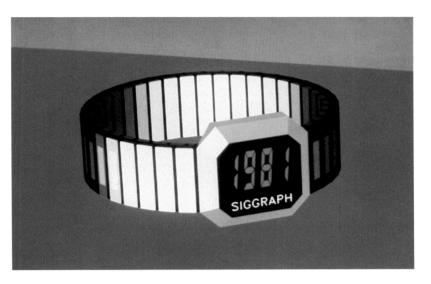

Realistic image produced with a Gaussian-shaped filtering technique. (Stuart Sechrest, Program of Computer Graphics, Cornell University, 1981.)

is jaggedness in line edges or in polygon boundaries.[25] Moiré patterns, the omission of small objects, and temporal aliasing artifacts (such as when wheels appear to spin backwards) are other examples.

One way of reducing the aliasing problems is to increase the sampling rate by increasing the image resolution. Aliasing is not eliminated but it is noticeably reduced. A more correct method is to filter the original function. For example, if an edge intersects the area defined by a pixel, the resultant color should be a weighted average of the colors of the two polygons on either side of the edge. A box filter uses a constant weighting and depends on the respective polygon areas overlapping the pixel.[26] Gaussian-shaped filters produce more realistic images (Figure 27). Until recently, these filtering techniques were too computationally expensive to be commonly used. However, if the filter's weighting function is stored in a look-up table instead of being computed for each pixel, the complexity of the filter does not affect the execution time and the computations are more rapid.[27]

A shadow is the darkness cast by an object intercepting light. It falls from the side opposite the source of light. Theoretically, when the observer's position is coincident with that of the light source, no shadows are visible. As the observer moves further away from the source of illumination, shadows become more visible.

The addition of shadows to a perspective image vastly enhances depth perception in the display. The shadows provide valuable positional information and improve the observer's ability to comprehend

25 F. C. Crow. "The Aliasing Problem in Computer-generated Shaded Images." *Communications of the ACM 20,* 1977, pp. 799-805.

26 E. Catmull. "A Hidden-Surface Algorithm with Anti-Aliasing." *Computer Graphics 12,* August 1978, pp. 6-10.

27 E. A. Feibush, A. M. Levoy, and R. L. Cook. "Synthetic Texturing Using Digital Filters." *Computer Graphics 14,* July 1980, pp. 294-301.

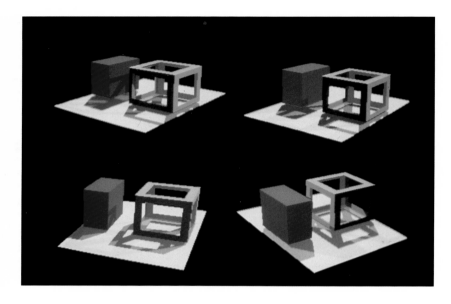

Shadowed image displays with multiple light sources. (Peter Atherton, Program of Computer Graphics, Cornell University, 1978.)

complex spatial environments. However, computation times and algorithmic complexity for shadow generation have prevented many implementations.

When ray-tracing methods are used, the generation of shadows is an automatic by-product, since objects that create shadows obscure the path of the view ray to the light source. For polygonal environments, two variations have been used.

Crow, in 1977, presented a shadow algorithm that calculates the surface enclosing the volume of space swept out by the shadow of an object, that is, its umbra.[28] The umbra surface is then added to the data and treated as an invisible surface which, when pierced, causes a transition into or out of an object shadow.

Perhaps the easiest procedure for casting shadows is based on a polygon visible surface algorithm, and consists of two parts.[29] Shadow descriptions are found by viewing the environment from the position of the light source. A hidden surface removed view from the light source position will delineate the shadowed polygons, which are those areas not visible. Once defined, these shadowed polygons are added to the original environment and treated as surface details on their original source polygons. Shadows can be created for any number of light sources and the resulting intensity effects cumulatively combined (Figure 28).

The realism of computer-generated images is enhanced when they simulate the texture or patina of a surface. Texturing is the ability to map these patterns onto the surface of a described object. The patterns

28 F. C. Crow. "Shadow Algorithms for Computer Graphics." *Computer Graphics 11*, Summer 1977, pp. 242-248.

29 P. Atherton, K. Weiler and D. Greenberg. "Polygon Shadow Generation." *Computer Graphics 12*, August 1978, pp. 275-281.

Brick texture tile mapped onto a polygonally defined object. A brick wall was photographed and a typical "tile" was extracted and then mapped in true perspective onto each polygon in the model. (Eliot Feibush, Program of Computer Graphics, Cornell University.)

29

Teapot with a geometric texture. (©Dr. James Blinn, University of Utah, 1976.)

might be variations in intensity and color, such as a wallpaper pattern or a photograph, or they might be variations in surface texture, such as the skin of an orange.

To create realistic images of these textures, and yet avoid a complete description of each minute element of the object surface, it is convenient to map the texture pattern onto the appropriate surfaces of the geometric model. Techniques are now available to simulate either intensity or geometric patterns,[30] and to map these onto either polygonal or parametrically defined curved surfaces.[31, 32]

In general, the approach is to define a source image or "texture tile," either mathematically or by digitizing an image into a two-dimensional array of intensity values. This source image must be sampled correctly, or aliasing artifacts will occur. When the source is composed of discrete values, it is customary to first filter or "blur" the information prior to sampling. The sample points are defined by geometric transformations relating the point on the object to the location in the source tile. Intensity values are again transformed or mapped to the correct position in the perspective image. Finally, intensity values are modified according to a convenient reflection model.

Two examples illustrate the power of this technique. In Figure 29, a geometric texture was mapped onto the teapot by perturbing the surface normals. Figure 30 shows how a digitized texture tile of a brick wall was mapped onto a polygonally defined environment as part of an architectural rendering system.

30 J. F. Blinn. "Simulation of Wrinkled Surfaces." *Computer Graphics 12,* August 1978, pp. 286-292.

31 J. F. Blinn and M. E. Newell. "Texture and Reflection in Computer Generated Images." *Communications of the ACM 19,* October 1976, pp. 542-547.

32 E. A. Feibush and D. P. Greenberg. "Texture Rendering System for Architectural Design." *Computer Aided Design 12,* March 1980, pp. 67-71.

Flight simulator scene of an aircraft carrier. (*Novaview* System, Redifusion Simulation and Evans and Sutherland Computer Corporation.)

Applications

An infinite number of applications can benefit from developments in computer graphics. The technology has moved so rapidly that it has outpaced our ability to apply it immediately. This section describes a few areas where computer graphics has already demonstrated its enormous potential.

Pilot Training

One of the first significant applications of real-time digitally generated raster images was in the training of commercial and military pilots, as well as astronauts. Displays of environmental terrain as seen from the cockpit of the aircraft are used. The simulations must be sufficiently real to provide all the visual cues necessary for pilot training, and they must be generated fast enough to simulate motion. Considering the immense amount of data necessary for a single image, one realizes that real-time image generation is a very demanding task. Special purpose, parallel and pipeline systems have been built to accomplish this, and although currently very expensive, they have been cost-effective and very efficient for pilot training (Figure 31).

Architecture

In architectural design, one of the greatest difficulties is understanding the full three-dimensionality of a project before it is constructed. Although architects may be trained to think spatially, their primary means of communicating their ideas to clients or engineering colleagues still consists of two-dimensional line drawings in the form of plans and elevations. Computer graphics techniques will radically change this design profession in several ways. Geometric modeling techniques will not

Architectural simulation on a digitized background.
(Kevin Weiler and Peter Atherton, Program of Computer Graphics, Cornell University, 1978.)

only allow more designs to be evaluated at the preliminary design stage, but will create a data base that can be shared by the cost-estimators and the mechanical and structural engineers. Drafting procedures can be completely automated, vastly reducing the work of producing construction documents. Finally, the construction of elaborate scale models will be replaced by the use of fully textured or shadowed images, set upon scanned backgrounds that can be video transmitted via interoffice communication systems (Figure 32). In the future, one will walk around a proposed building before the construction documents are started, and even these documents will be stored on and accessed from machine-readable magnetic tape.

Structural Engineering

Interactive computer graphics is responsible for dramatic changes in structural engineering analysis and design. The widespread availability of computing power and the formulation of computerized stress analysis routines during the last three decades have revolutionized the profession. Almost all stress analysis applications, such as building structures in architecture; engineering vehicle dynamics in aerospace, automotive, or shipbuilding; the production of pressure vessels and mechanical parts; and geotechnical engineering, now use finite element methods of analysis.

The finite element method utilizes a set of simply-shaped, interconnected elements to represent a complex object. From these models are derived structural equations that specify the contribution of each element to the total system response. When the contributions of individual components are combined, the behavior of complex structures can be predicted.

33

Finite element mesh of a Gothic church cross-section.
(Dr. Mark Shephard and Dr. Robert Haber, Program
of Computer Graphics, Cornell University.)

34

Color display of stress levels after analysis. (Dr. Mark
Shephard and Dr. Robert Haber, Program of Computer Graphics, Cornell University.)

The extremely voluminous and complex geometrical and topological information required to describe three-dimensional problems
can now be generated via interactive computer graphics. Preprocessors,
which prepare the input data, vastly reduce the time required for input
and also result in greater efficiency, since the graphic feedback reduces
input errors. For example, Figure 33 shows a graphical vector display
of the input data for the analysis of a two-dimensional cross-section of
a Gothic church, a task normally requiring many hours but performed
in minutes using a finite element preprocessor.

Just as important will be the use of postprocessors, which display,
in color, the results of the stress analyses to the designer. Instead of
attempting to comprehend and evaluate masses of numerical data,
the engineer-designer can immediately visualize the structural behavior
using color-coded representations of the stress parameters. Figure 34
shows the stress contours after the structure has been analyzed. The
availability of pre- and postprocessors will inevitably allow the designer's creative judgment to be inserted into the iterative design process.

Medicine

Computer graphics systems are being increasingly used to present bio-
medical information for medical research, diagnosis, and treatment
planning. A computer system's ability to combine information from
two-dimensional images, such as x-ray photographs, fluoroscopes, or
tomographic scans, into a full three-dimensional representation, can

36

Three-dimensional medical image obtained from CAT scans. This three-dimensional description was obtained by using "lofting" procedures, and can be viewed from any direction. All of the positional and volumetric information is known. (Alex Sunguroff, Program of Computer Graphics, Cornell University.)

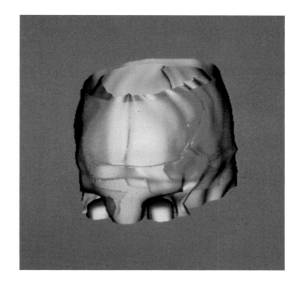

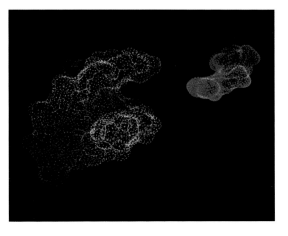

35

Drug molecule, Netropsin, fitting into the groove of DNA. (R. Langridge, T. E. Ferrin, R. Schaefer and M. L. Connolly, Computer Graphics Laboratory, University of California, San Francisco.)

provide the medical profession with a new vision into the human body. In fact, using computer graphic reconstruction methods, noninvasive techniques may in time significantly reduce the need for exploratory surgery. The following examples illustrate some of the pioneering research efforts currently being conducted.

At the University of San Francisco School of Pharmacy, color computer graphics, on vector displays, is being used to model molecular structures, and the means of attachment of various drug molecules (Figure 35).

At Columbia University, neuroanatomical studies involve the use of serial sections to examine specific nerve structures and structural changes. Using tomographic information obtained from CAT scans, serial sections can also be combined to create three-dimensional surface representations of human organs (Figure 36). Perhaps even more importantly, the tomographic information can be used to plan radiation treatment strategy for cancer patients.

Cartoon Animation

The use of computer graphics in cartoon animation is perhaps one of the most highly publicized application areas. The traditional method of creating motion in an animated sequence requires the animator to draw a large number of pencil drawings with gradual or exaggerated variations from one figure to the next. These pencil sketches are xeroxed on transparent celluloid, and then painted with an opaque paint to complete the finished "cel." Background paintings are separately created for each scene. A single frame is created by overlaying the separate "cels" on the background painting and filming the composite image with an animation camera. The entire animation process is extremely labor-intensive, and rising labor costs are substantially increasing the production expense.

Several computer-assisted approaches can be used. One popular method is called *key-frame in-betweening*, where the key-frames are drawn or traced into the computer and the computer performs the interpolation. A second method is to scan each pencil sketch into the computer. Almost all applications now use the machine to assist with the opaquing process and to automatically assemble and merge the images to create the animated sequence. Since animation is the art of exaggeration, this author prefers to leave the creative process entirely in the hands of the artist, and rely on the scanning method only. Figure 37 shows one frame of a scene from Hanna-Barbera's "Fred Flintstone" series. The image was interactively colored and automatically merged after the pencil sketch was digitized. Recent developments now allow the simulation of multi-plane cameras and special effects. If these techniques are used properly, the quality of animation can be enhanced significantly in the future.

37

Computer-generated cartoon animation. (Marc Levoy and Bruce Wallace, Program of Computer Graphics, Cornell University.)

Conclusions for an overview article of an emerging field are always inconclusive. Obviously, the technology in terms of both hardware and software has reached the stage where it is useful in a large variety of disciplines. The reduced costs of computer memory and computer processing, and the availability of mass-produced television technology clearly allow computer graphics displays to be used economically. More significantly, pictorial communication is necessary because we live and think in a visual, three-dimensional world. Computer graphics provides this medium of communication, one which can establish a symbiotic relationship between the user and the machine, and allow humans a greater opportunity to harness the awesome computational power of the machine.

The question is no longer whether one should use computer graphics, or even when one should use computer graphics. The most challenging problem is how our society can use these methods most beneficially. By reducing the barriers of communication, our capabilities for problem solving and information dispersion will be greatly enhanced. To quote Ralph Waldo Emerson, "An idea whose time has come is the most potent of all natural forces."

Computer Art

South Temple. 1981. ©David Em.   *Navajo.* 1979. ©David Em.

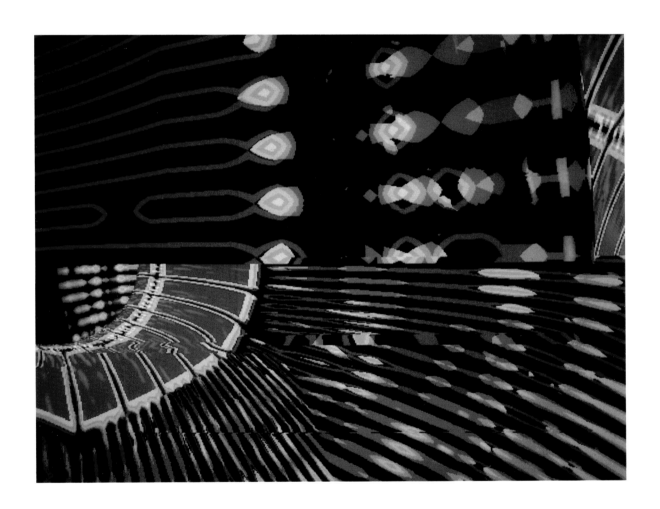

Larry 2. 1979. ©David Em.

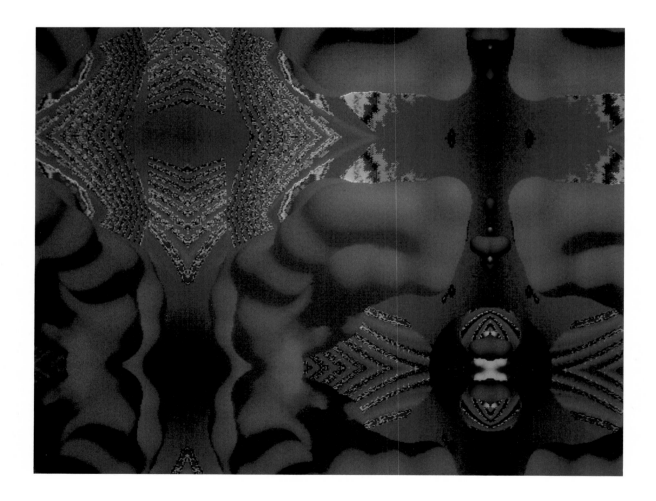

Omomo. 1980. ©David Em.

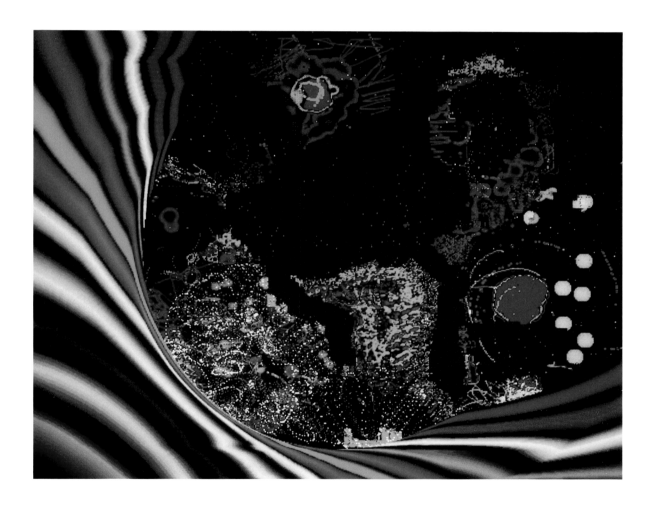

JSDD #2. 1980. Joel Slayton, Visible Language
Workshop, Massachusetts Institute of Technology.

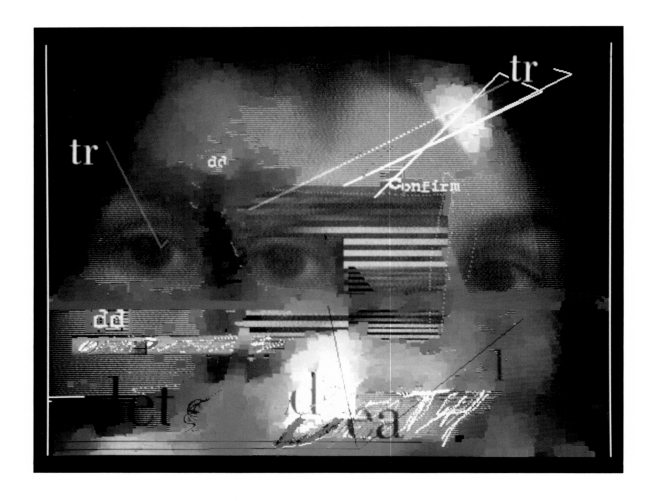

JSJS. 1982. Joel Slayton, Visible Language Workshop, Massachusetts Institute of Technology.

San Francisco. 1981. Darcy Gerbarg, Aurora Imaging
Systems.

Pt. Richmond. 1981. Darcy Gerbarg, Aurora Imaging Systems.

David Weimer, Bell Laboratories.

Turner Whitted and David Weimer, Bell Laboratories.

Scenes from Computer Animated Films

Voyager II image recorded during its trip past Saturn.
Dr. James Blinn, Jet Propulsion Laboratory.

Adam the Juggler. Richard Taylor, Craig Reynolds,
Mal McMillan, and Art Durinski, Information
International, Inc.

X Wing. John Whitney, Gary Demos and Art Durinski,
Information International, Inc.

Television commercial for Scientific American. Advertising Agency: Marsteller, Inc. Digital Effects.

The Works. Artists: Dick Lundin and Lance Williams.
New York Institute of Technology Computer Graphics
Laboratory.

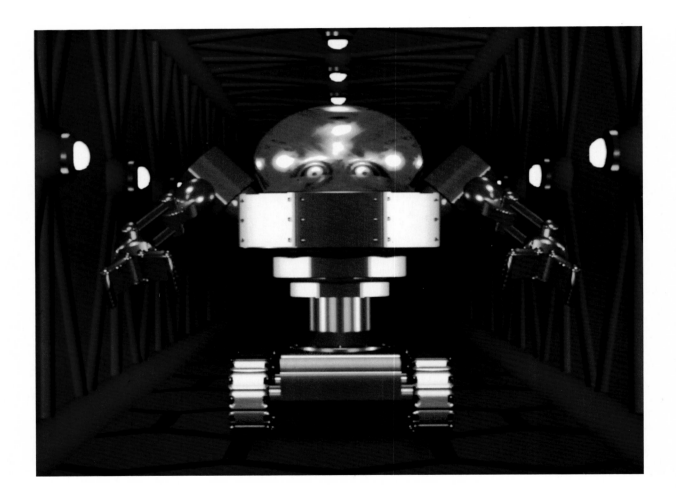

Scenes which simulate different times of day. Nelson Max, Lawrence Livermore National Laboratory.

Synthetic Landscapes

Landscapes created with fractal surfaces. Loren
Carpenter.

Views of Aspen, Colorado. Walter Bender, Architecture Machine Group, Massachusetts Institute of Technology.

Models of Molecules

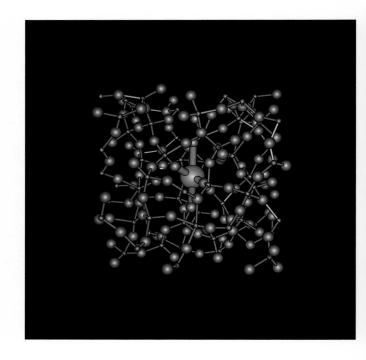

Tomato bushy stunt virus. The bottom subunits of the model have been removed to show the underlying structure of the virus.

Neodymium laser glass. The glass is a random network of beryllium and fluorine around a neodymium ion (the green sphere).

Twenty base pairs of B-DNA. The colors represent the different types of atoms in the double helix.

Six base pairs of DNA with the drug molecule Ethidium Bromide in place.

All, Nelson Max, Lawrence Livermore National Laboratory.

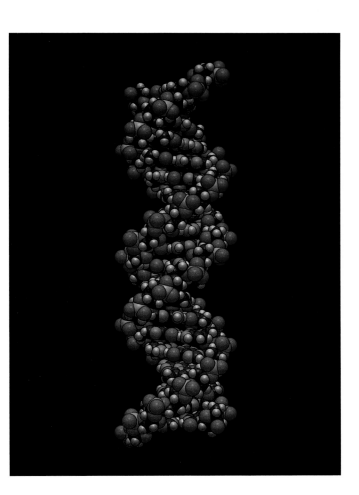

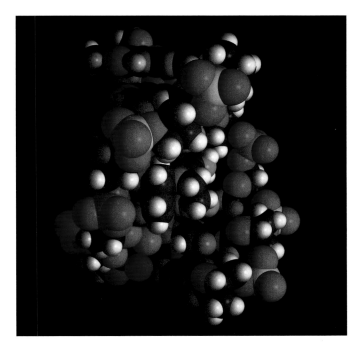

Computer-Aided Design

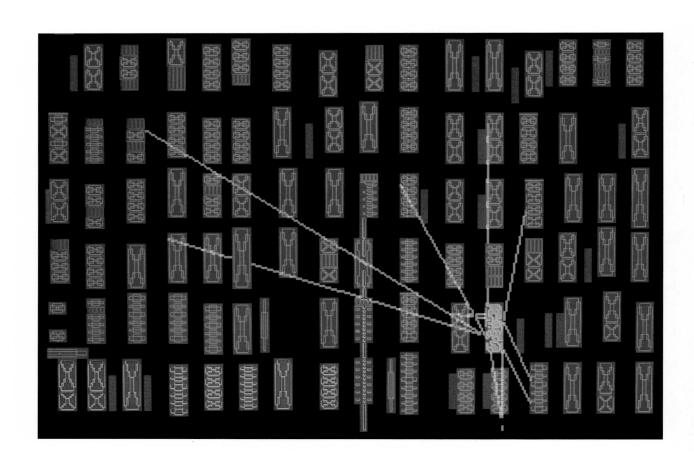

Design for placement of integrated circuits on a printed circuit board. Honeywell Information Systems.

Model of two-thirds of an automobile body mount. Ford Motor Company.

Model of one-half of a 5-bolt automobile wheel. Ford Motor Company.

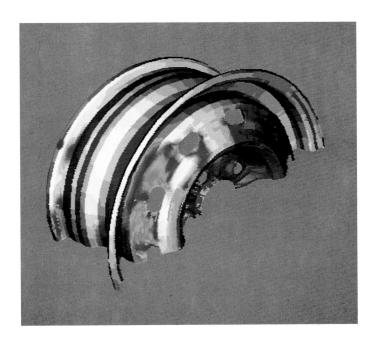

Solid modeling of a gearbox. Center for Interactive
Computer Graphics, Rensselaer Polytechnic Institute.

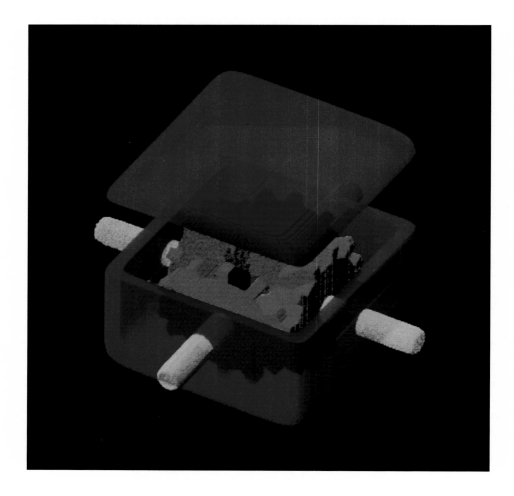

Oriental rug. Designed by the Van Heugten Company of the Netherlands. Lexidata Corporation.

Piping design for a refinery. Calma Company.

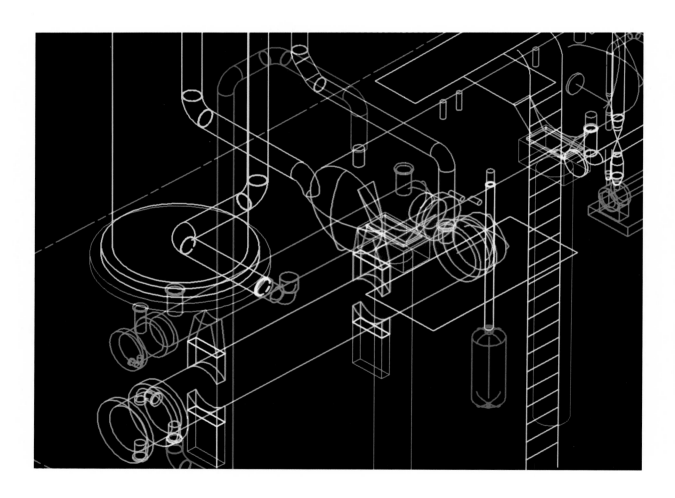

Integrated circuit. Calma Company.

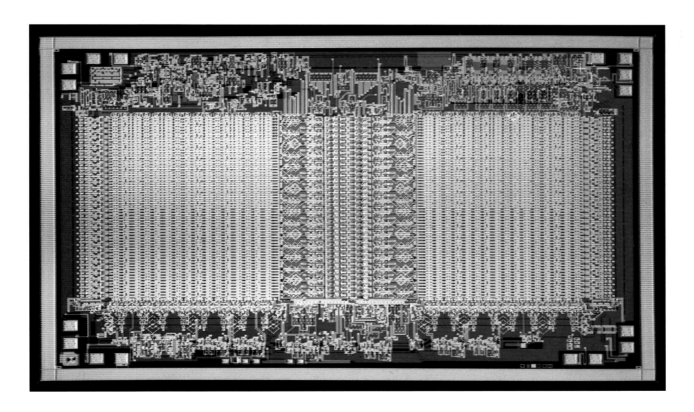

Simulation of a high velocity impact upon a test material. Bruce Brown, Lawrence Livermore National Laboratory.

Model of a high energy explosion within a steel canister. Bruce Brown, Lawrence Livermore National Laboratory.

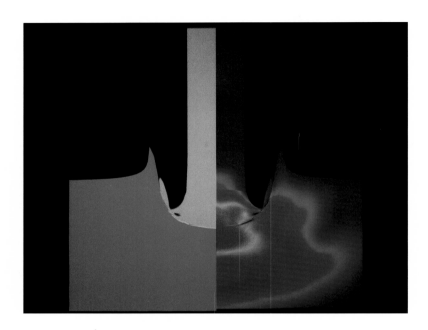

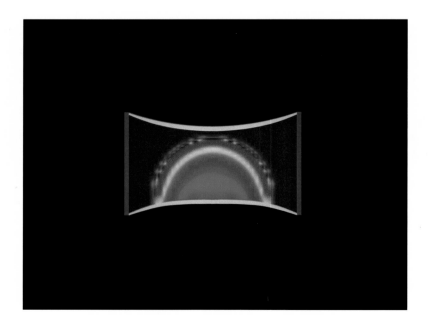

Remote Sensing

Land use image (1980) of the Mount Monadnock region in New Hampshire. Information was compiled from existing maps, field surveys and Landsat satellite imagery. Denis White, Carl Steinitz and Douglas Johnston, Harvard University Graduate School of Design.

BARE ROCK
LAKES, PONDS
RIVERS, STREAMS
WETLANDS
SOFTWOOD FORESTS
MIXED FORESTS
HARDWOOD FORESTS
FORESTRY—SELECT CUT
FORESTRY—CLEAR CUT
RECREATION
AGRICULTURE
SUMMER HOUSING
EXISTING HOUSING
LOW DENSITY HOUSING
HIGH DENSITY HOUSING
UNPAVED ROADS
2—3 LANE ROADS
LIMITED ACCESS ROADS
INTERCHANGE
COMMERCE
INSTITUTIONAL
INDUSTRY
RAILROAD

Weather satellite image of a hurricane over the Pacific
Ocean (pseudo-color). International Imaging Systems.

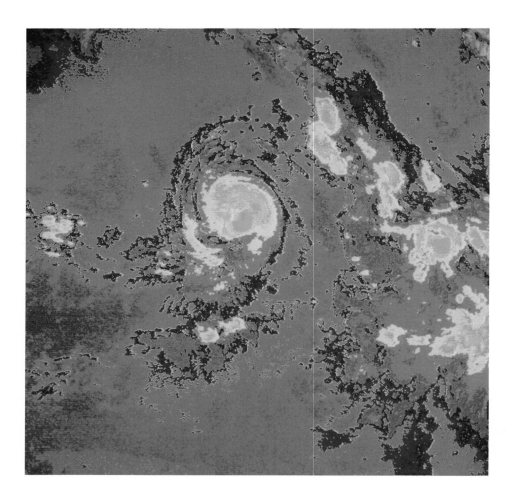

Thermal infrared image of the Mount St. Helens vol-
cano some three months after its eruption. The data
was acquired with a Daedalus digital multispectral
scanner from an airplane. Red areas indicate the highest temperatures. United States Department of Energy's
Remote Sensing Laboratory, operated by EG&G, Inc.

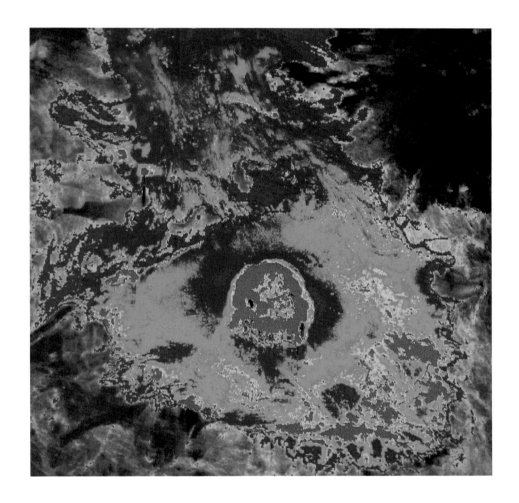

Landsat satellite image of the Grand Canyon area of
northern Arizona with the Colorado River on the right.
International Imaging Systems.

Landsat satellite image of the Paraguay River north of Asuncion, Paraguay. The dark blue area represents water; light blue is shallow water; dark green is upland forest; light green is lowland forest; brown is grasslands; and yellow is open land. Environmental Research Institute of Michigan, Earth Resources Data Center.

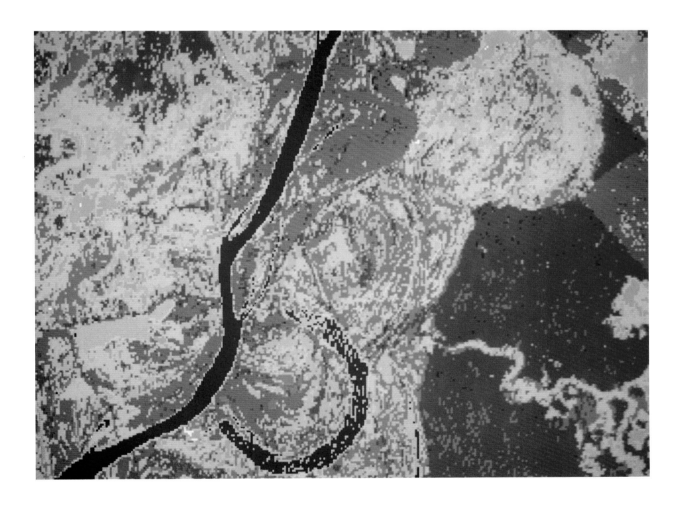

NIMBUS-7 satellite image of the northeast coast of
the United States. The green area off Cape Cod represents the Georges Bank region with its high concentration of chlorophyll; the bright blue spot south of
Cape Cod is a warm eddy separated from the Gulf
Stream. Dr. Otis Brown, Dr. Robert Evans, Dr.
Howard Gordon, and Mr. James Brown, University
of Miami.

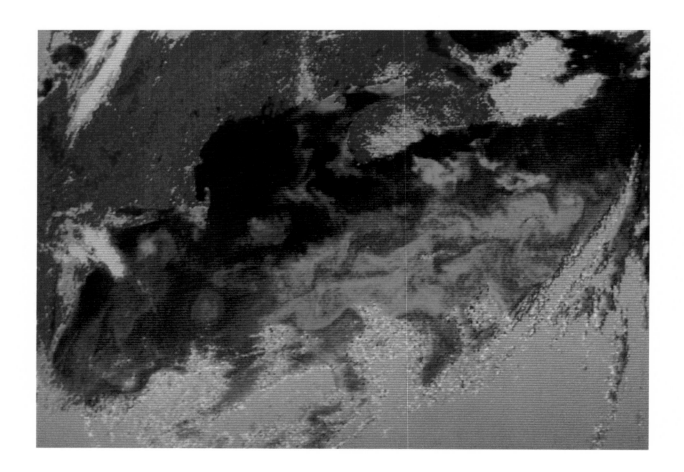

Martian landscape recorded by the Viking 1 Lander
Module (color enhanced). Regional Planetary Image
Facility, Department of Earth and Planetary Sciences,
Washington University, St. Louis, Missouri.

Astronomy

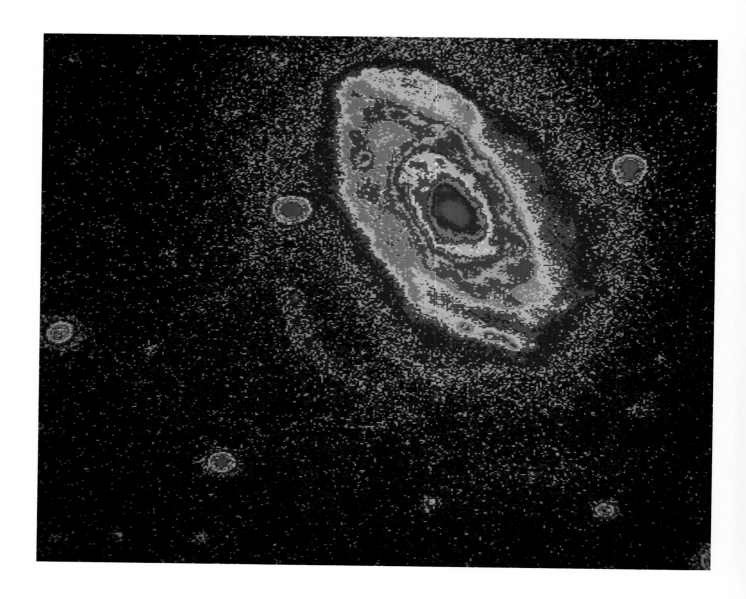

Magnitude 13.5 galaxy (pseudo-color). The original data was recorded on a photographic plate with the Mayal four meter telescope at the Kitt Peak National Observatory. Dr. John Jarvis, Bell Laboratories.

Infrared image of the Orion Nebula (pseudo-color). The original data was recorded at the NASA Infrared Telescope Facility with a charge-injected two-dimensional array built by the NASA Goddard Space Flight Center. Harvard-Smithsonian Center for Astrophysics.

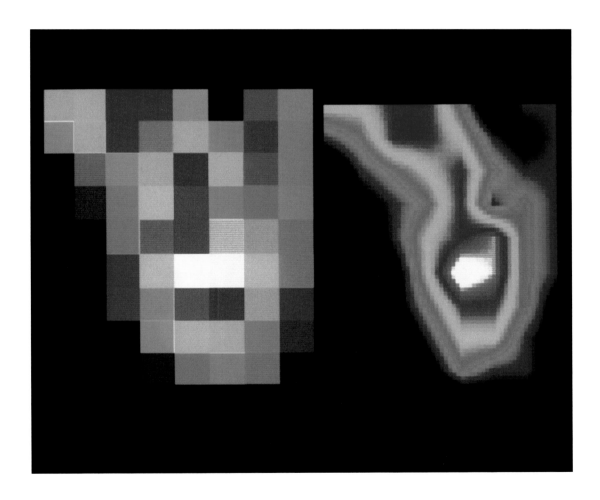

Color: A Tool for Computer Graphics Communication

AARON MARCUS

Color is a rich and powerful component of our daily lives, appealing to our senses, our intellect, and our emotions. Beyond its ability to evoke a physiological response in us, color can influence our mental state and may even affect our physical condition. Cultures, religions, and societies have nurtured strong, often indelible associations of color that can operate at an unconscious level.

We assume it is natural that we should have strong feelings about certain colors. Sometimes, we can choose which colors we will use to communicate about ourselves to the world. We select the colors in the clothes we wear, deciding to dress conservatively or fashionably. Often, our response to color is the result of many unconscious influences. The color of clothing and cosmetics provokes an instant response, favorable or unfavorable, with us. Architecture, sculpture, painting, and graphics delight or disturb us with their use of color. We react quickly and efficiently to color coding in familiar settings: We stop at a red light and go on green.

The experience of color, although not always conscious, is a potent one. To the person inexperienced with its use, color is influential, mysterious, and seemingly uncontrollable. In the earliest civilizations, every person contributed to the creation and use of color. As society became more differentiated, high priests of color emerged; artists and designers became skilled in the discipline of color. In today's "post-industrial" society or "information age," the situation is similar to earliest times in terms of color. Modern technology has placed within the hands of the average person the ability not only to receive color (printed publications, television, and so on), but to create color and to communicate with it. Nowhere is this truer than in the world of computer graphics.

Computer graphics systems allow users to design their own color worlds and to communicate color to others. In the fields of word processing, typesetting, chartmaking, map making, computer-aided design, and image processing, many people without expertise in color theory

I

Josef Albers. *Homage to the Square: Glow*, 1966, acrylic on fiberboard, 48 x 48. Hirshhorn Museum and Sculpture Garden, Smithsonian Institution, Washington, DC.

and practice are now in a position to do their work in color. From an artist's and designer's perspective, the most that can be said of much computer graphics output is that it is colorful; however, it appears to reflect a lack of serious decision-making about color. To really use the power of a computer graphics system, we must understand more precisely how color aids communication.

Color can be a toy: Something for fun and amusement. Or color can be a tool: One of several visual symbols that helps inform, persuade, and appeal to readers and viewers. In the highest sense, the artistic sense, color can also be a totem, that is, a revered entity deserving of respect, devotion, and care. Embodying this approach to color is the work of Josef Albers (1888-1976), one of this century's greatest color artists, theoreticians, and teachers. In Figure 1, *Homage to the Square: Glow*, 1966, Albers uses a composition of extreme simplicity to explore subtle color relationships. For such artists, the interaction of colors is a revelation through which one can better understand the phenomena of the rest of the world. Color becomes a universal symbol.

Most users of computer graphics systems can learn from the artist's and designer's approach to color. In the remainder of this article, I intend to clarify some issues about color as it relates to the output forms of computer graphics. I shall discuss the merits of color, color terminology, and phenomena, the artist's and designer's approach to color, and some general strategies. No fixed prescriptions can be made; color is not that simple, but a set of observations can significantly enhance a user's appreciation for differences in color combinations and skill in manipulating color selections.

We shall cease to think of color as a mere toy, a cosmetic addition to our lives; we may not go so far as to worship it as an end in itself, but we shall definitely understand it as a tool to help us communicate.

Color as a Tool

What can color do? What are its merits as a tool of communication? Research has demonstrated that color can enhance communication, although it is difficult to explain precisely how it does this. We know, however, that color can accomplish the following:

It can help portray natural objects and processes more realistically, thus making the display of information more believable, appealing, or comprehendible.

It can depict the logical relations between ideas, that is, logical structure; and it can portray abstract processes or temporal structure. In a complex display, this may be extremely valuable to efficient communication.

It can call attention to specific data or information.

It can help label or identify parts or elements of structures and processes.

It can help reduce errors of legibility or interpretation. For example, consistent color coding of primary and secondary information may simplify the reader's (or viewer's) search for information.

It makes available more dimensions for coding data and it permits perceptual separation of closely spaced data in text, table, chart, map, or diagram presentation. It can help a viewer absorb information, reach decisions, and take action more quickly.

It can enhance the appeal or readability of a display. This can be especially important in convincing an audience of uncommitted viewers or in a situation of information overload.

It can help make a display more memorable to the viewer by providing additional cues for information retrieval.

While color has many advantages as a tool for communication, it also has certain drawbacks. The wise user of color in communication should be aware of the following limitations:

Color invariably requires more expensive display systems and distribution media.

Color blindness places a distinct limitation on the efficacy of some color coding. Approximately 8.5 percent of males and 0.5 percent of females suffer from some form of color blindness.

Displays of too-strong color may cause eye fatigue with prolonged viewing or may even cause confusion. In such situations, color may increase, rather than reduce, reading errors. This can occur in slide presentations with too strong a contrast in the colors or in video or cathode ray tube (CRT) displays.

Because color is such a complex and potent medium, it is easy to inadvertently misuse it. For example, errors can occur because of improper grouping of unrelated but similarly colored elements.

There may be strong emotional reactions to the use of color. In some groups, the use of color may be regarded as frivolous or ostentatious. Accountants, for example, are oriented toward a black-and-white numerical world and may view the use of color with skepticism. These reactions may change with increasing acceptance of color graphics.

Some groups may have arbitrary, but strongly negative reactions to the use of particular color. During the 1972 Olympics in Germany, for example, the graphic design group responsible for color selection avoided color combinations that were typical of the previous German Olympic games, held during the Nazi period.

Cross-disciplinary or cross-cultural influences on color interpretation may induce undesirable cognitive or emotional reactions. For example, European choices for male or female colors vary greatly from American Indian preferences. Among technical professions, there may be differences over what should be considered

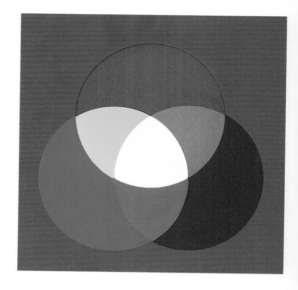

2

An additive mixture of luminous primary colors blue, green, and red. Note that mixtures become increasingly lighter in value as more light is added, eventually reaching white in the center.

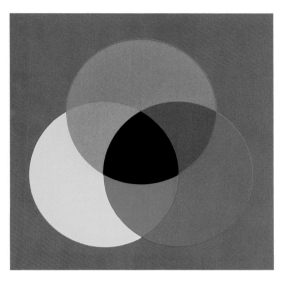

3

A subtractive mixture typical of colored pigments in painting or of inks in printing. In this optical mixture from printing, a complete black mixture is not achievable with the standard process printing primaries cyan, yellow, and magenta. The screening process used to achieve mixtures is purposely exaggerated to make the mixing technique more obvious.

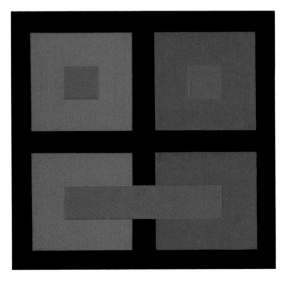

4

Simultaneous contrast showing a change of hue.

"standard" color codings. For example, city planners often use violet or purple to signify industrial activity; many industrialists would not, however, associate these shades with industry.

Often, the advantages of using color outweigh the disadvantages. The question then arises: Which colors should one select and how should they be used? To make sense of professional guidelines, it is necessary first to understand some of the basic terminology, structure, and processes of color display.

Basic Color Phenomena

There are two ways to understand and describe color phenomena: In technical terms (how it is produced, how the human visual apparatus works) and in psychological/aesthetic terms (how it is perceived, how it is interpreted cognitively and emotionally). In order to discuss the perception of color, I shall first summarize some of the technical details of interest to the user of color computer graphics systems.

The spectrum of visible light occurs in the range of 400 to 700 nanometers (nm), from violet to red, but pure spectral colors are rarely seen except in the rainbow or when separated by a prism. Most light sources project a combination of wavelengths. Most substances absorb a substantial portion of incident light, reflecting a mixture of wavelengths. Thus, most color is a polychromatic phenomenon, not monochromatic or of pure wavelength. A spectrophotometer can measure incident light or the portion of incident light reflected from a substance, and the measurements produce a characteristic spectral distribution curve for the color. Perceived color is a complex mixture of these spectral characteristics and the human processing of color information. Perceived color can be described in several ways. For our purposes, hue, value, and chroma are appropriate and easily understood.

Hue

Hue is the attribute represented by the infinite combinations of different wavelengths. This attribute is what most people are referring to when they use the term *color*. Hues can be ordered in a number of different ways, for example, according to their progression in the spectrum. Primary hues are those which, when combined, can produce all other combinations. Luminous or light-emitting color sources create additive combinations. These can be expressed as combinations of the additive primaries; blue, green, and red light, which create white when mixed equally (Figure 2). Color reflected from a surface can be expressed as a combination of the subtractive primaries cyan (blue), yellow, and magenta (red). When mixed in equal combination, they produce a dark (ideally black) composite color (Figure 3). A hue's appearance is strongly influenced by its surroundings. The measured and the perceived hues may therefore not correspond. Note the illusion of three hues appearing as four in Figure 4. This occurs because of the effect of the surrounding color on any given color.

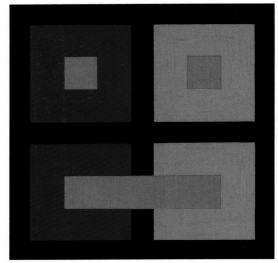

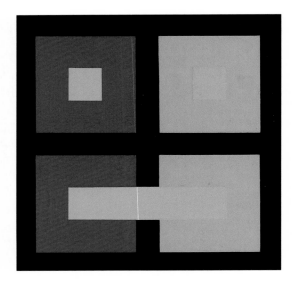

5

Simultaneous contrast showing a change of value.

6

Simultaneous contrast showing a change of chroma.

Value

Colors are light or dark in value. Value is the perceived (as opposed to measured) lightness or darkness of a color. Luminous light sources vary in their brightness or in the amount of luminous intensity per unit area. A color's measured lightness (also called *luminance*) is not the same as the color's *value*. As with hue, the apparent value of a color is affected by its surroundings. Note the illusion of three values appearing as four in Figure 5. Reflected colors vary in their reflectance, that is, in the ratio of reflected light to incident light. The amount of energy present in a color, whether it is from a light source or reflected from a substance, is the lightness of the color.

Chroma

Colors are vivid or dull. The third basic attribute of color, *chroma*, refers to its saturation or its purity, that is, the amount of gray in the color. This dimension of color designation is often difficult to describe and identify, since for many reflective substances and light sources chroma is linked to value. A high chroma or vivid color can be made weaker or less vivid in two ways: (1) by mixing in gray or (2) by mixing in the complement of identical value. As with hue and value, the surrounding environment can affect the chroma of a color. Figure 6 illustrates how a single figure on two different backgrounds creates an illusion of four colors.

Specification

There are several systems for designating colors. The CIE system (Commission Internationale de l'Eclairage) is based upon measurements by instruments and the physical characteristics of light. Neither CIE nor the red-green-blue (RGB) system (suitable for video or CRT displays) has all the characteristics desirable in a color specification system. While some systems are difficult to understand intuitively, others are difficult to measure. One system, the Munsell color system, is based upon perceptual experience of reflected colors and is widely used in industry and government. It is the system to which artists and designers most easily refer, and it is the basis we shall use in this article. The Munsell color solid identifies a color in terms of hue, value, and chroma (Figure 7). Each of these dimensions is divided into perceptually equal steps: Hues into 100 steps, values into 10 steps, and chroma into approximately 16 steps. Actual color chip samples of more than 1500 (reflected) colors constitute the basis of the system. Using the analogy of the globe, the system measures values along the north-south axis. The axis itself is an achromatic scale of grays (including black and white). Hue is measured around the equator and in planes parallel to the equatorial plane. Chroma is the distance out from the north-south axis to a particular

7

The Munsell color system. Courtesy of Munsell Color, Baltimore, Maryland.

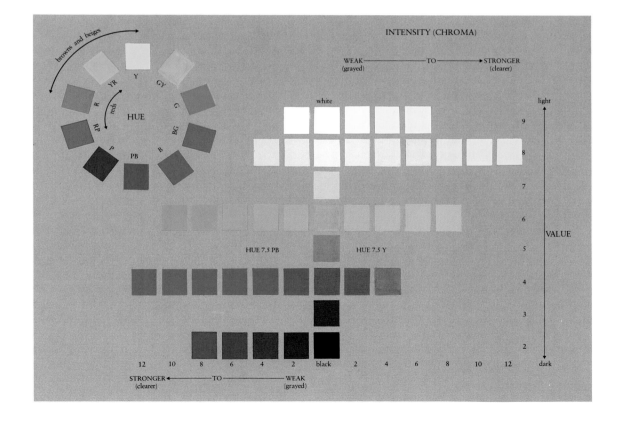

82

The systematic arrangement of hues, values, and chromas in the Munsell color space. Using the analogy of the globe, white is at the north pole, black at the south, values would be equivalent to latitude, and hue would be equivalent to longitude. Chroma would measure the distance from the north-south axis.

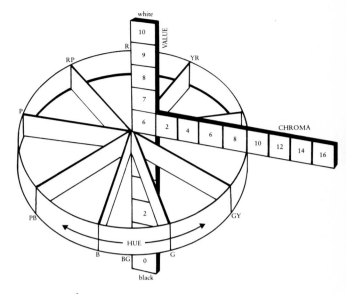

7b

The plane of 100 equally spaced hues of which the five principal hues are red (R), yellow (Y), green (G), blue (B), and purple (P). The five intermediates add to these to make the 10 major hue groups, each 10 steps apart.

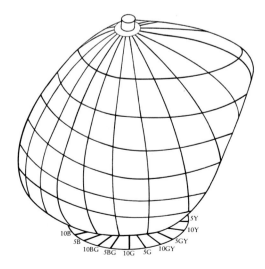

7c

The irregular three dimensional shape of the Munsell color space.

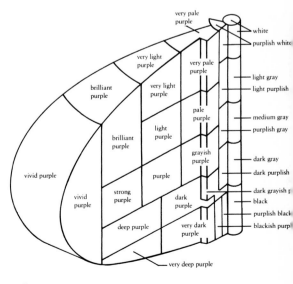

7d

A cut-away of the Munsell color space near purple and the color name scheme proposed by the National Bureau of Standards.

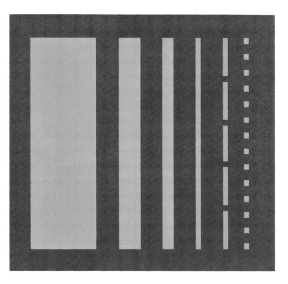

8

Color change due to the amount of color in a plane, a line, and a point.

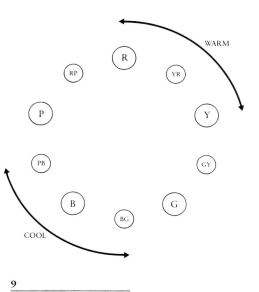

9

Warm versus cool colors. The arrows are only approximate since variations in value, chroma, and surrounding context can affect the color "temperature."

color. Colors become progressively grayer as they move in toward the center. Note that the Munsell color solid is not a regular form, but is a spheroid distorted because of the physical limitations of materials.

Two advantages of the Munsell system are its widespread use in various commercial and service sectors of the economy and its relative ease of comprehension. The National Bureau of Standards has developed a color language terminology based on this system. By using standard terms like "dull" and "vivid," "light" and "dark," together with suffixes like "-ish," as in reddish, and composite words like "blue-violet," this terminology permits us to refer fairly precisely to particular parts of the Munsell solid without using a complicated numerical classification.

Color Interaction

Knowledge of the basic terminology of color is useful but not sufficient for artists and designers. They spend considerable time in school and in professional practice learning about the complicated interaction of colors, how a particular color is affected by its color environment within a composition. As we saw in Figures 4, 5, and 6, the foreground colors are affected by the background colors in which they occur. Changes of hue, value, and chroma are possible. This means that one cannot just choose individual pretty colors, but must consider how these colors will interact. Look again at Figure 3, in which the foreground color turns bluish on the red background and reddish on the blue background. The red background seems to remove some of the red from the red-blue (purple) foreground color. The quantity of a given color can also change its apparent hue, value, and chroma. In Figure 8, the same color is presented in several different formats. This suggests that typographic characters composed of small linear strokes may appear to be a different color than a large flat area of the same color. These changes may occur inadvertently in various color compositions such as charts, maps, diagrams, and textural displays. Users of computer graphics systems must experiment to determine whether they are inadvertently creating undesirable color change effects.

The artist and designer create distinctive compositions through contrast, harmony, and rhythm. These phenomena can be interpreted in color terms through the selection and manipulation of varying hues, values, and chromas.

Contrast

One kind of color contrast is the opposition of warm (red, orange, and so on) and cool (blue, green, and so on) colors (Figure 9). We tend to notice the warm colors, which seem to be more active, and to jump forward from a neutral (gray) environment toward the viewer. The cool colors, on the other hand, seem to sit further back and are somehow more passive and stable. The terms *warm* and *cool* are not strictly defined, be-

10

Giorgio Morandi. *Still Life,* 1960, oil on canvas, 12 x 18.
Collection of Graham Gund.

cause colors are affected by their environments: What is warm in one environment may appear cool in another environment.

These contrasts in hue are often apparent in interior design, clothing, and works of art. Representational painters, for example, often use warm colors to accent dark or cool interior scenes or landscapes. Landscape painters routinely make more distant objects bluer to mimic aerial perspective. Another obvious example is the portrait, in which the warm face emerges from a dark neutral or cooler background. Some painters are noted for their particular use of warm colors or cool colors in their work. An example is Pablo Picasso (1881-1973) who during his "blue period" painted many canvases with variations of that hue.

Another kind of contrast is that of value and chroma rather than hue. Whenever there are strong controlled variations in value and chroma we tend to read them as spatial differentiations. Such light and dark variations are normally used to imply illuminated and shadowed areas of three-dimensional objects. Landscape painters have traditionally utilized such contrasts to enhance the impression of space, which their works convey by making more distant objects appear duller. Such light and dark contrasts also lead the eye around a composition. This approach in painting is called *chiaroscuro.* Value creates an effect of spatial location. Light colors often tend to appear nearer while dark colors recede. There is a strong tendency for the viewer to attribute heaviness or weight to low value colors and to attribute light weight to high value colors.

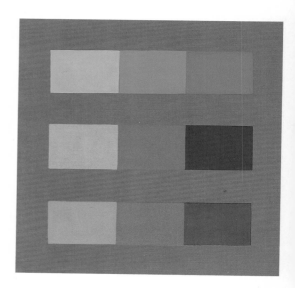

11

Monochromatic color harmonies achieved by changing the value.

Harmony

Harmony is the sense of relatedness among colors. For example, a monochromatic set of colors changing only in value (dark red, red, and light red) has an immediately perceived relationship that seems clear and natural. Figure 10 shows a 1960 painting, *Still Life*, by Georgio Morandi (1891-1964), who typically used closely related low chroma colors to establish a quiet, thoughtful mood, a mood not unrelated to that needed when examining complex information.

Traditionally, multiple hue harmonies have been established through selections of colors on the circle of hues that are close together (Figure 11), opposites (complementary colors) (Figure 12), or near opposites (split complementaries) (Figure 13). Theoreticians of color have proposed other regular geometric patterns overlayed on the hue circle to determine harmonious sets of colors. Whenever determining color harmonies, it is best to be able to examine a set of colors of equal size in some simple grouping such as a straight line placed on a neutral background field (gray) or on another color that may be used in the graphic image.

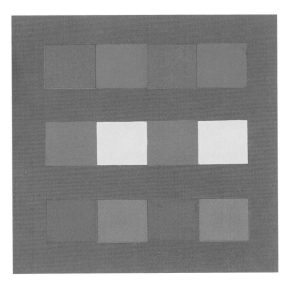

12

Approximate complementary color harmonies based on the Munsell hue circle. Subtle changes of hue and chroma can affect the strength of the combination. Note the vibrations at the borders where the colors meet.

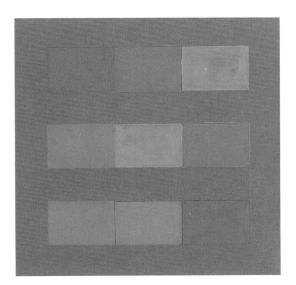

13

Approximate split complementary color harmonies based on the Munsell hue circle. Subtle changes of hue and chroma can affect the combinations.

Rhythm

Although such mechanical selection of colors can exhibit harmonious relationships, it can also lead to disturbing vibrations along the boundaries separating them, for example, combinations of vivid red and green or red and blue. The final visual rhythm of a composition is determined not only by what colors are selected but also by the relative amounts of each color and their spatial arrangement. Together, these factors can produce a sense of static balance or of asymmetric balance in which our eye is attracted in directed movement to various colors within the composition. Balance is achieved by organizing the amount and location of colors as well as their hue, value, and chroma. Consider a simple example, such as the balance of colors established in *Broadway Boogie Woogie*, 1942-43, by Piet Mondrian (1872-1944) (Figure 14). In keeping with the aesthetic interest of the time, his colors are primary hues. They are distributed in a simple arrangement on the surface in a clearly defined grid. Mondrian suggests, through color, the urban bustle of New York City and the syncopated music of that time. Not everyone has Mondrian's sense of color. Often, when we look at graphs, charts, or maps, we find that poor color choice leads the eye to focus on inappropriate or insignificant elements of the communication.

Color Guidelines

Having discussed color phenomena abstractly, we need to look at more specific and concrete examples of decision making in the use of color. We are focusing primarily on information-oriented images, although the image output by computer graphics systems runs the gamut from informational to persuasive to aesthetic communication. Informational images such as charts, maps, and diagrams can be used in business management, in data analysis for science and mathematics, and in structure or process monitoring for engineering.

Color guidelines for persuasive and aesthetic graphics cannot be easily listed; they are formed after long experience. Principles for color selection in the display of significant data, however, are more easily identified. These principles apply equally well to the design of charts, maps, diagrams, tables, and texts.

Most professional graphic designers, chartmakers, and cartographers follow three basic principles.

1   They use color only with great care, and some even caution against its use—especially for the representation of quantitative changes.
2   They limit the use of different colors. Although we can perceive millions of colors, we cannot keep track of more than a dozen when we have to remember them and distinguish them in a pattern. In fact, five to seven different colors appears to be a more workable limit for many situations of color coding. Multicolored charts or maps generally create confusion. General goals are to have consistency of color choice and to make the colors as distinguishable as possible.

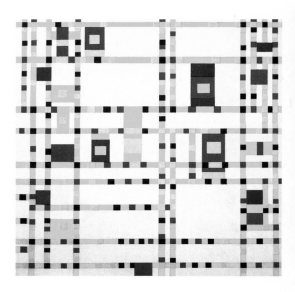

14

Piet Mondrian. *Broadway Boogie Woogie*, 1942-43, oil on canvas, 50 x 50. Museum of Modern Art, New York.

3 They give the most important elements in a chart, map, or diagram the most important color and the greatest contrast with the background.

There are other principles specifically related to hue, value, and chroma.

Principles of Hue Selection

Hue selection should take account of the viewer's generally poor color memory and a likelihood of some color blindness. When used to distinguish elements, hues should be as different as possible from one another. Our sensitivity to hues is ranked approximately in this order: Red, green, yellow, blue, purple. Because perceived color changes with respect to background and with respect to the perceived size of the colored elements, background color in the figure-field relationship must be considered. This is often overlooked when colors are selected. With other factors being equal, the eye can more easily resolve detail in monochromatic images. Background colors that mix several colors (for example, brown) make it harder to distinguish fine detail. Another factor that decreases hue distinguishability is simultaneous contrast (see Figure 4). This means that in the patchwork multihue situation typical of maps, for example, nearly identical colors may be misread due to the immediate color contexts in which they appear.

Some hues look more unique and distinctive than others. They enter the culture as basic color names. Researchers have shown that this depends upon a given culture and its language at a moment in history. One authority lists blue, green, yellow, red, brown, black, and white. These unique hues should be used when symbolizing distinctly different items, for example industrial and residential areas in a map. Apparent color mixtures should be used to symbolize the fact that certain referents share in some attributes, for example, a yellow-green area in a diagram would indicate the presence of both the yellow and the green items.

Because hues are associated with moods, social structures, and cultural activities, it is important to determine if these can be used constructively for a given audience. One list of such associations appears in Dreyfuss' *Symbol Sourcebook*. Some hues are more favored than others by a given audience. This may be a significant factor in effective communication. One authority maintains that Western culture prefers blue, red, and green, in that order, giving lower ratings to orange and yellow.

Principles of Value Selection

Value is the most significant color dimension in terms of legibility (distinguishability). Color value differentiation is more readily preserved if an image is produced in a degraded form or reproduced in another medium, for example, a color painting reproduced in a book. Nevertheless, our recall and recognition of a particular value is limited. For this reason, quantitative indexing of value should be limited to approximately five steps. As noted with Figure 5, the phenomenon of simultaneous contrast changes the apparent values and may cause confusion.

In some maps, charts, or diagrams, it may be necessary to create a regular sequence of gray values from light to dark, possibly including white and black. Our eyes respond differently to differences among dark or light colors. This logarithmic response to barely noticeable differences is called the *Fechner law*. Accordingly, the difference between 10 and 20 percent gray areas will appear smaller than the difference between 60 and 70 percent gray areas. In order to make a sequence appear regular, an irregular selection of gray values must be used. Figure 15 shows an example of the Munsell equal value scale, which is often used to determine a set of equal gray values. Note that complex interactions within a map may still affect the sequence and disturb the regularity. When seeking to create a graded series of colors, try to do so through a sequence of grays or values of a monochromatic hue rather than a spectral hue sequence. One researcher has shown that a progression of values communicates temperatures in maps more efficiently than does a two-hue series with strong connotative aspects (such as red and blue to convey warm and cool).

A connotative aspect of value is that value changes imply magnitude changes, that is, dark values on a white field invariably imply more of whatever attribute is being symbolized. Sometimes this effect may be at odds with the communicator's intent. Likewise, extreme values tend to dominate a graphic display. Therefore, large contrasting areas may attract attention to semantically empty areas of the display. An example would be a map of the world's continents appearing on a white page in which the oceans contrasted more strongly with the page color than did the land masses.

In relation to typography, value is especially important. Because of the size of characters and their linear nature, value is one of the strongest determinants of legibility. Although many colors may be available, only a few will be suitable for presenting extensive text material (more than a paragraph). In limited color palettes, such as eight colors in a two-bit color display, only white, yellow, and green may be suitable for text among the display colors seen against a dark field.

Principles of Chroma Selection

The dimension of chroma is the least useful in quantitative display. Chroma differences are usually tied to value differences for a given hue and display materials.

One aspect of chroma that the user can consider is that we usually associate higher magnitudes with higher chromas. Another point to bear in mind is that the larger the area of color, the more chroma it will appear to have. Thus, color selected from a small area sample may be misleading. This is extremely important to anyone selecting color for a background as opposed to color for small typographic or cartographic symbols. The viewer may confuse two similar hues or two values of the

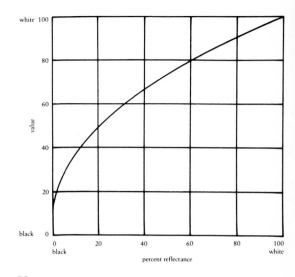

15

The Munsell equal value scale. It shows that percentage differences in low (dark gray) reflectance make relatively large differences in value. At the opposite end of the scale, differences in high (light gray) reflectance make relatively small changes in value. Where grays are prepared in equal 10 to 20% intervals, the perceived value difference between 10 and 20% will be noticeably smaller than the perceived value difference between 70 and 80%.

same hue having essential differences of chroma because large areas of the lower chroma color may appear similar or identical to small areas of the higher chroma color.

As mentioned earlier, researchers have proven the existence of innate, cross-cultural associations of certain meanings with certain colors. High chroma colors are associated with happiness, strength, and goodness, while low chroma colors are often associated with despair, weakness, and evil. However, a designer should avoid a too simplistic interpretation of these associations. A single color association is not necessarily the most important color statement of a visual image. The overall effect needs to be considered. Individual colors can't be selected without seeing the entire palette together.

Color Precision

We have briefly discussed several factors in color selection but have not mentioned pattern, textured surface, glossiness, and other attributes that can have a significant impact on the apparent color. These factors must be considered in the design of color compositions. Color precision is especially complex when the designer is creating color compositions interactively on a display screen for later viewing in hardcopy form. Currently, in most computer graphics environments, there are no means for creating identical colors as one moves from the CRT image to hardcopy output. Many color images are reprocessed for mass distribution in a form other than the first generation hardcopy format. Color prints or color plots may be rephotographed for use in magazines, or slides may become color xerographic prints. Often it is almost impossible to check the final form to ascertain that color fidelity, legibility, readability, and impact are preserved. The best principle to follow is to try to simulate the final viewing conditions in terms of materials and illumination when creating the computer graphics display.

Many display terminals require that the user make considerable effort to create a stable, calibrated color display. The red observed today may not be the red seen yesterday, because someone else may have re-adjusted the color controls. It may be difficult to regain the exact color settings. Always remember that certain colors of a composition need to be more finely tuned than others. For example, viewers are very sensitive to flesh tones in representational human images but can more easily tolerate wide variation in other colors.

A color composition viewed in daylight instead of in fluorescent light can have drastically altered color relationships. It cannot be assumed that the colors suitable for a presentation on a white page will be suitable for display on a slide in a darkened room. The most important principle the designer follows here is to be aware of the differences and to experiment with several combinations before making a selection. Although the computer graphics system may not make it easy, you should try to view the palette of colors against the final background color, with no other color distractions. If some colors will be used only as point or linear elements, they should be viewed as such in conjunction with the other colors.

How to Get Started

For every kind of color computer graphics system, it is important to have some homemade standards to help in judging color harmony and fidelity of reproduction. Using whatever capabilities the system has, try to produce a simply organized, controlled set of variations of many or most of the system's colors. Show them as small color swatches and, if convenient, as line and point elements.

Use some standard test images of the kinds that you typically produce as a basis for investigating means of reproduction. Determine how an image produced at a terminal or on a hardcopy device will appear as a Polaroid print, as a 4x5 color transparency and/or negative, as a 35mm lecture slide, as a color xerographic print, even as a black-and-white image screened for printing or simply as a black-and-white photograph or xerographic print. By retaining some standard images in a file with information about how they were made, observing the results, and noting what happens, it is possible to develop some guidelines for effective use of color based on actual systems.

In terms of developing harmonious color relationships, the best advice for a given project is to experiment with two to three variations of a proposed set of colors. Show them to potential viewers or even colleagues to get feedback on their harmony and legibility. Most importantly, make a decision among alternatives which you can actually see, not between a combination that is before you and some unseen but imagined improvement.

This summary of principles of color design should be viewed only as a primer, a way of getting started in the exploration of color. Even for professionals, experience with dynamic color and easily changeable color palettes are new conditions. Our knowledge of the impact of computer graphics systems on the design of texts, tables, charts, maps, and diagrams is only now evolving. Computer graphics systems present us with a revolutionary capacity to generate dynamic color symbols in space. Skillful attention to the use of color in our own culture as well as in other cultures and historical periods will help us realize the full potential of color computer graphics systems for improving human communication.

Computer-Aided Business Graphics

ALLAN H. SCHMIDT

Computers vastly increase the rate at which data is available, but that data's usefulness is still constrained by the ability of the human mind to extract information from a flood of numbers and words. In order to make data more comprehensible and to reduce the time required to extract useful information, computer graphics techniques are being developed that allow us to perceive information in the form of visual images. Some of these images are similar in appearance to traditional presentation graphics. They are significantly different, however, in the methods used to prepare them, the purposes for which they are prepared, and the results they achieve.

The power of computer graphics results from a synergy between the computer's ability to store, manipulate, and display data as numbers, words, or pictures, and the human's ability to recognize and interpret patterns in data presented graphically.

This essay provides an introduction to the emerging world of business graphics, including a brief review of the changing role of graphics in business; examples of current applications; and a description of the hardware, software, and data bases required to use computer graphics. Ways of getting started in the use of computer graphics are discussed. Finally, future uses of computer graphics in business, government, education and the home are outlined.

The Changing Role of Graphics in Business

Numbers, Words and Images

Most individuals absorb information presented orally in a rigid, sequential fashion from one source at a time. In contrast, information that can be presented graphically with minimal use of numbers or words is rapidly absorbed and is retained by the mind as an integrated set of patterns. The ease with which we remember and recall visual images as opposed to words or numbers has led to many theories which describe human mental processes as involving image manipulation and pattern recognition.

Automation of Engineering and Presentation Graphics

In business, some activities make extensive use of information in the form of graphic images, but the majority make little or no use of graphics as a means of communication. Engineering and manufacturing are activities that are dependent upon graphic communication. One study at Boeing Aircraft estimated that a typical engineering document contains 30 percent graphics, 65 percent text, and 5 percent numbers. Other common forms of business graphics include gant charts and network diagrams used by managers for the planning and monitoring of projects. Senior managers and executives also use graphics for presentation purposes.

Computer-aided design and drafting (CADD) technology has significantly increased the productivity of design engineers and draftsmen. Its use is common in the electronics, automotive and aircraft industries. In many applications, a CADD system will pay for itself in less than one year through savings realized from increased worker productivity.

A second area in which savings have been realized is that of presentation graphics. Computer graphics and composition systems can help the artist prepare charts, graphs and their accompanying texts. Once again, productivity is increased by the use of electronic drawing, composition and reproduction aids. The equipment is similar to that used in the design and engineering departments. In these applications the operators are creating and manipulating electronic images of physical objects (CADD) or of statistical data which has been selected for use in a presentation or publication.

Beyond CADD and Presentation Graphics

Recently, computer graphics have begun to be used for detecting, interpreting, and communicating information critical to the management of an organization. Business graphics may be descriptive, analytic, or persuasive.

Descriptive graphics are used as a visual summary for repetitive management reports. Such reports and their companion graphics are used to monitor performance (for example, productivity or quality control) within an organization or to compare the performance of several divisions. Such graphics are data driven, that is, their purpose is to summarize data contained in recurring reports.

Analytic graphics are idea driven because their purpose is to represent information about a specific issue being studied. Such graphics are produced as part of special projects—for example market research studies—undertaken to identify potential problems or opportunities and to evaluate alternative courses of action. Analytic graphics typically involve several iterations where initial displays provide insights to a problem and suggest the need for additional displays. Computer graphics makes it possible to prepare and evaluate a series of alternatives in a short period of time.

Persuasive graphics are used to support a point of view and as such are decision driven. This is the domain of traditional presentation graphics which are commonly used in executive briefings where a specific proposal is being recommended for adoption. Computer-generated graphics also allow for the use of descriptive, analytic and persuasive data in a decision support environment. For example, descriptive graphic displays would document a situation and a variety of related information such as changes over time. Analytic graphics would follow to help identify and evaluate alternative courses of action. Persuasive graphics would then be used to highlight the reasons why one alternative is superior to all others and should be or has been adopted. Decision support graphics are used by product managers, product line management committees, project review committees—anyone with responsibilities for strategic decision making.

Visual Thinking

The use of computer graphics to support management decision making assumes that data traditionally reported in numeric form is often more valuable and meaningful if it can be "seen" in an appropriate graphic format. When the data are presented graphically, the following effects are achieved:

1 Data reduction. An immediate summary of the data is visible.

2 Error detection. Abnormally high or low values in the data are immediately apparent.

3 Exception reporting. Deviations from plan or projected values become obvious.

4 Comparative value. Significance of the data can be established by displaying a second set of graphic data to allow for comparison. Bar charts and pie charts are graphic techniques that make such comparisons.

5 Trend analysis. Direction and magnitude of change are apparent when data from different points in time are displayed graphically. Graphs of many types can provide information on such trends as rate of sales, company growth, and so on.

6 Correlations. The degree of similarity or difference for two or more data items is apparent when techniques such as scatter plots are used. Examples include plots of volume sold versus size of discount, or education versus salary.

7 Spatial relations. Data that includes locational references are often impossible to interpret unless they are shown in a graphic form such as a map. A company's ability to understand its market location and penetration, and so on, is substantially improved by the use of maps produced via computer graphics.

For each type of graphic, the information already exists, but the graphic description points out significant patterns that otherwise are likely to go undetected.

Applications of Business Graphics

Marketing and finance are two areas in which business graphics have experienced rapid growth. Described below are marketing and financial applications that use computer generated graphics.

Marketing

Computer graphics are being used to identify the location of existing markets and also to increase the effectiveness of a company in reaching those markets. The location and extent of a company's current sales activities become immediately apparent when data describing current customers are displayed on a computer-generated map. Other maps can be prepared showing the location of a total potential market using data from a commercial data source. Valuable information concerning sales performance, market penetration, market share, and market opportunities can be derived from such graphics. Site location studies, the location of markets for advertising purposes, measurement of market penetration and analysis of market potential are described in the following examples of current applications of computer-generated maps.

Site Location

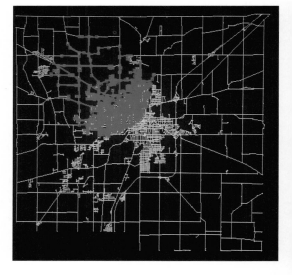

The selection of sites that minimize transportation is increasingly important because of rising fuel costs. Recent studies demonstrate the ability to evaluate alternative sites for either their accessibility by customers, such as for a shopping center, or their accessibility to customers, as in the case of a delivery dispatching center. Computer graphics used to evaluate accessibility from a distribution center to all locations within a region is shown in Figure 1. A city street network was analyzed to identify all minimum paths, shown in yellow, extending out from a potential origin to possible destinations. This study was conducted by a major department store and involved use of a computer program known as NETWORK developed at the Harvard Laboratory For Computer Graphics. An earlier application of the same program had been carried out to evaluate the relative accessibility of alternative sites for wholesale fish markets within Seoul, Korea.

General Motors is pioneering in the use of computer graphics in its dealer survey program. In order to reduce the field work involved, computer maps are being prepared showing the location of all new car registrations for each division plus the location of each dealer in a particular city. Similar maps are prepared showing the location of competing models and their dealers. The data are available from the R. L. Polk Co. which each month publishes a data base of all new car registrations. In addition, demographic data are plotted by census tract areas. Since each map is produced on transparent mylar, they may be overlayed to permit easy identification of the sales penetration by specific manufacturers and dealers. The size of the maps allows them to be superimposed on standard road maps to orient the reader and also to indicate the location of major transportation routes and other features. Inspection of the maps

1

allows one to evaluate current dealer performance and the need for additional dealers or relocation of existing dealers. The technique will let General Motors reduce its field surveys for data collection and instead use field work to verify interpretations or to spot-check questions. In addition, General Motors expects to consolidate dealer survey programs currently performed by each division into a single corporate survey.

Yamaha Corporation has used computer mapping in its dealer survey programs for several years to help its dealers locate their markets and to assess the need for new or relocated dealers. Their applications involve the preparation of maps showing the distribution of Yamaha motorcycles sold by each dealer as well as each dealer's location. The computer then plots a boundary around the region in which the closest two-thirds of each dealer's sales occurred. Based upon a map of total market potential, a second boundary is drawn to indicate where a comparable number of sales could have been made with a focused sales effort.

Market Potential

Major corporations are turning toward strategic marketing by drawing on their particular strengths relative to the competition and focusing on a specific industry using people on their staff who know how to communicate with that industry. *The New York Times* has developed a data base of the top ten thousand corporations and used computer graphics to help its corporate advertising clients identify the regional location of specific industries. Working with Design Systems Research, Inc., the *Times* has analyzed fifty-five industry groupings and has produced graphics showing what percentage of each industry's headquarters and of each industry's total sales volume are located in various regions of the United States. After compiling the data, John Rawson, Advertising Manager for the *Times* found that "numerical tables just overwhelmed people. With computer graphics, we don't use numbers. It is often sufficient to just show relative importance, one region of the country compared to another." His data base can be used to illustrate the fact that although 70 percent of the oil and gas extraction companies have headquarters in the South, their sales only account for 19 percent of the United States total. Whereas, the 12 percent of the oil companies with headquarters in the Northeast account for 54 percent of the industry's sales. Corporations using business book advertising to reach company executives in any of the fifty-five industry markets can quickly visualize their location using the data base and graphics prepared by *The New York Times*.

Scandinavia World Cruises uses computer graphics prepared by Demographic Research Co. to target its marketing efforts with travel agencies. Using customer demographic profiles plus demographic data from the U.S. Census, they prepare weekly maps of zip code areas illustrating how each sales office is performing relative to its forecast.

Their salesmen prefer the graphics because they now receive a map showing the location of travel agents and the zip code areas of high customer potential rather than a thick report.

Market Penetration

Dunn's Marketing Service, a Division of Dunn and Bradstreet, uses computer graphics to deliver market analysis data to its customers. Drawing upon the Dunn and Bradstreet information resources which describe over eighty percent of all United States businesses, Dunn's Marketing Service is able to help a client firm identify the number and location of its potential customers. Gary Harmon, Dunn's Product Development Manager, says that their use of computer graphics has substantially increased the value of the reports which they prepare for a customer. "Computer graphics are startling in their effect," said Harmon. "They have formed a bridge between having information and being able to understand and act on it. Previously, the client was almost buried in computer output. Now, he can literally see his firm's potential markets." Computer maps produced by Dunn's are used to illustrate the distribution of a client's potential customers by county within a state or by state within the United States.

Cable television companies are very interested in the distribution of current and potential customers in their franchised metropolitan areas. Early cable television services within an area depend on locating the maximum concentration of potential subscribers and installing the minimum amount of cable. Warren Steiner of Warner-Amex Cable Television points out that the use of computer maps permits comparison of actual penetration with market potential in a metropolitan area, and also helps field people plan for future expansion. The demographic characteristics of potential customers are well-known and their location by census tract can be displayed on a map that uses 1980 Census data.

Computer graphics prepared by Geographic Systems, Inc. were used to determine current and potential markets for the consumer products division of a major corporation by ESG Associates, an economic consulting firm. They analyzed the extent of market penetration for a particular product in various parts of the United States and were able to determine how the penetration might be increased by reallocation of marketing and sales resources. Using data aggregated by Sales and Marketing Information (SAMI) regions, ESG prepared a series of computer maps showing such factors as: the rate of growth for total market of plastic wrap and bags; the rate of growth for total personal income (a factor well-correlated with the sales of plastic wrap and bags); and a correlation of growth of total market with growth in personal income.

Elliot Grossman of ESG explains that "the areas with low market growth and low income, or high market growth and high income do not represent areas of high potential. These areas are performing at their potential. Regions with high market growth and low income growth are performing above potential, and are likely candidates for having dollars in sales effort reallocated away from them. Regions with low market growth and high income growth are the candidates to receive dollars from the other regions just mentioned."

Finance

Financial data provide the ultimate indicators of the success or failure of management's performance. As a result, financial reports for each division of a firm as well as an entire corporation are closely monitored by both management and investors. Income and expense are regularly evaluated in relation to current objectives, prior performance, operations of competing firms, and the national economy. Data for several time periods are examined to identify trends and to project future conditions. Various key factors are also computed and displayed as a means of evaluating resource allocation and the resulting performance in relation to corporate objectives. Graphic standards take on particular significance because of the critical importance of accurate financial reports. A growing number of individuals are concerned with the potential distortion of financial data when it is shown in graphic format. This problem results from the lack of a standard graphic format which can be used consistently for data describing a specific subject but reported by different individuals. The following application describes a computer-aided graphic technique for producing financial statements and other data driven reports in a standard format. Examples of financial trend analysis and the use of computer graphics by an investment advisory service are also discussed.

Graphic Financial Statements

Corporate annual reports frequently include one or more charts indicating changes in earnings, and earnings per share over the past ten years. Recently, such information as complete balance sheets and income statements have been displayed in a graphic format. Irwin Jarrett, an accountant, has begun providing such computer-generated graphics to his clients in a standard format. Jarrett reports that his clients find graphic financial reports more valuable because of their ease of interpretation. The graphic techniques used are based upon principles of Cuisinaire rods commonly used in the "new math" of primary education. The resulting graphics look like horizontal bar charts. Jarrett has used this technique to present information normally contained on an income statement or balance sheet and to portray both financial position and selected critical ratios. Dale Inman of Digital Equipment Corporation has applied Jarrett's approach to presenting nonfinancial data such as manpower allocations, costs and other management reports.

Financial Trend Analysis

Business decisions often require a knowledge of past trends. Graphs representing data collected over time can illustrate past trends, while mathematical extrapolations of that data can estimate future trends.

There are many statistical procedures available to produce such estimates; computer graphics permits quick conversion of the statistical projections into graphic models. However, assumptions formed from projections based on short- and long-term trends need to be carefully evaluated. For example, the disaggregation of time-series data for several items into individual trends can significantly alter the interpretation of an initial projection. Figure 2, produced by Computer Pictures, Inc., illustrates how initial estimates of projected sales for product A were substantially revised. Because its short-term trend indicated a downturn from its long-term trend, plus a decline relative to sales of other products, a revised projection lowered the original estimates of future sales.

MCI Telecommunications recently began providing its senior management with graphic reports of key factors related to corporate financial performance. Joel Shapiro of MCI said that his goal is "to provide for senior management a rapidly assimilable picture of the company on a continuing basis. We have learned the significance of vertical versus horizontal views of data. It has always been necessary to know how we have done the past month but there is a great deal of value to look across time and be able to say this is where we are improving or where we are not improving. That information gives us an ability to manage by exception, so we are able to apply additional emphasis in areas where we are not performing as well as we could. We are using graphics as a fine-tuning tool for a fairly well run organization."

Senior managers at MCI can page through a data base of previously stored graphic images using a touch sensitive display screen and a menu driven hierarchical retrieval procedure. The graphic data base is continuously updated with new images being produced and stored automatically as part of a library of graphic images. Figure 3, produced by Computer Pictures, Inc., illustrates past and projected MCI expenditures for its management information system (MIS) operation as a percent of total revenues.

Investment Analysis

Mark Raclin, Executive Vice President of Lowry, Raclin, Harrell and Howerdd is using computer graphics to provide investment advisory services to pension fund managers and other members of the investment community. Raclin believes that "virtually every investment manager in America can prove that he is doing an outstanding job," because no standard definition exists for measurement of performance by investment funds. His firm is developing a set of criteria by which pension fund consultants can evaluate both their own performance and that of various pension fund investment alternatives. Criteria used include comparative data such as corporate finances, mergers and acquisitions, application of cash and cash flow, endowment spending programs, asset mixes, types of securities, and so on. This data base, which filled ten three-ring notebooks and thousands of pages of computer printout, is now being converted to graphics. Ultimately, Raclin intends to de-

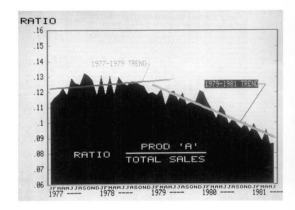

2

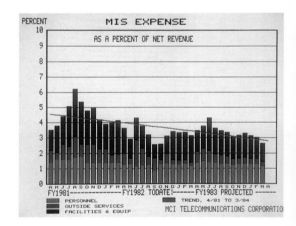

3

velop a library of graphic images that he can analyze and retrieve on demand. When a pension fund consultant requests information concerning a specific security, Raclin will be able to retrieve the images pertaining to that company from a floppy disc and provide them to his client.

Raclan declares, "computer graphics will be a complete revolution for us. The charts and tables we used to make with an art studio were usually generic in form, rather than derived from a dynamic model. Taking a stack of numbers to an artist and asking him to make any sense out of it was impossible. When I went to a graphic artist with numbers, I told him what the picture should look like and he made it look like that. This will no longer happen. Now we can see what the numbers look like on the screen and perform some relatively sophisticated analyses. Trying to describe multiple regression analysis with words and numbers is difficult, but with computer graphics, it's easy. Graphics have become a working, dynamic tool for examining data. Graphics are the only thing a client really understands."

The marketing and financial applications described above have several recurring benefits:

> They provide graphic representation of information not apparent in the numerical data
>
> They meet the highly diverse information needs of a broad range of users in many different industries
>
> They use data derived from internal corporate data bases as well as from external proprietary data base vendors
>
> They provide a diversity of graphic formats: black and white, color, two- and three-dimensional, and so on
>
> They evoke a high degree of satisfaction and enthusiasm on the part of the user

Having described the changing role of graphics in business, we will next discuss the resources required and alternatives available for getting started in the use of business graphics.

Resources Required

The resources required to create computer graphics are similar to those needed to produce manual graphic displays. They include technical tools (hardware), procedures (software), selection of specific graphic formats and symbols, plus a set of data to be displayed. In addition, graphic standards are needed to support interpretation and communication of the resulting graphic.

Hardware

The required computer hardware must be able to produce graphic images as well as manipulate and display numbers and text. Graphics may be displayed in black and white or in color on a cathode ray tube

(CRT). These displays may be output to paper or film at widely varying speed and costs. The graphics may be stored on magnetic tape or disc as electronic images for later display, modification and printing. Graphic arts quality output usually requires specialized and expensive computer graphic hardware. However, many applications, including most data driven graphics for internal use, can be produced with lower aesthetic quality but equivalent information content, using far less expensive graphics systems. For example, matrix printers primarily intended for data or word processing are often quite satisfactory. The compromise is in the acceptance of slightly jagged diagonal lines and a lack of color. However, when graphic arts quality is required for publication or presentation purposes, the desired graphic quality can easily be recreated using more specialized equipment available elsewhere within the organization or at a remote service bureau that specializes in such work. Either the images themselves, or the data base from which they were derived, can be transferred from one system to another via magnetic tape or telecommunications.

Software

Computer programs (software) are the critical ingredient that provides the hardware with the intelligence necessary to create graphic displays, or perform data and word processing. Computer graphics programs tell the hardware how to construct graphic formats and symbols. These programs allow a user to select specific types of graphic formats (such as bar charts, pie charts, maps, and so on); in addition, they display symbols, numbers and text as part of the final product. For data driven applications, computer graphic software is relatively fixed once a graphic product has been defined and is to be produced on a recurring basis. Software to support idea driven applications requires more flexibility because it will be used as a general-purpose tool that can be tailored to changing requirements. For example, mapping software must be able to display geographic boundaries such as counties, zip codes, or sales districts for a selected region as well as display symbols, and colors that represent data values at those locations for any available subject.

Data Bases

Data used to produce business graphics may be the operating statistics of a company or they may be obtained from external commercial data base sources such as Dunn and Bradstreet, Data Resources, or National Planning Data Corp. Regardless of source, data must be in machine readable form (such as magnetic tape or via telecommunications) or else they must be entered into the system through a keyboard. An existing data base management system can be used to produce a separate data file to be used independently at a separate graphic arts work station.

Market research studies frequently require special tabulations of data from both internal and external sources. Proprietary data for use in such studies are becoming available on a wide range of topics such as industry profiles, econometric forecasts, demographic data, and so on.

Computer-generated maps of sales districts, census tracts, zip codes, or other boundaries require a cartographic (x-y coordinate) data base (CDB) defining the regions of interest, such as sales territories. These data bases can be purchased from commercial, governmental or university sources. A CDB serves as a template in that the boundaries are predefined and the data values from a separate statistical data base are displayed as dots, shading, color, or other symbols on the map.

Graphic Standards

The effectiveness of business graphics depends on the use of graphic standards reflecting consistency, simplicity and style. Graphic symbols communicate information and are the vocabulary of a graphic language. As in any language, there must be consistency in the meaning of the basic elements and of subsequent combinations. Consistency of design, formats, symbols, colors, type fonts, and so on is essential in business graphics; otherwise, it would be difficult if not impossible to compare two or more graphic displays. The differences in such displays should be attributable to differences in information content, not to variations in graphic structure or symbolic vocabulary.

Conventions for business graphics should be developed on a company-wide basis. Graphics prepared at different times or by different divisions can then be interpreted on the basis of a common graphic language. The selection of graphic conventions presumes that there are data definition and reporting standards within an organization. A good example of data definition and reporting standards is that used by the accounting profession for financial reports. These reports are defined as to purpose, content, and structure and are well-suited to the use of consistent graphic conventions.

Business graphics should be simple in design to allow the reader to isolate and focus attention upon one unknown at a time. Perception of pattern is maximized when each display focuses on a single idea or subject with a minimum of visual clutter. To use graphics for data reduction or summarization of many different subjects, it is best to produce several displays—each dealing with a single subject—and then to do additional composite graphics when necessary.

Graphic style should reflect the "information culture" of the intended recipient. Individuals at various levels of a corporation are likely to have different expectations concerning the packaging and presentation of information. Differences in graphic style will be an issue when information is intended for distributon beyond the group that prepared or initially received a graphic. Peer group graphics require less refinement than those for "external" distribution.

Computer graphics that are available for distribution outside a company raise the issue of corporate image. Because of their enduring visual impact, graphics can have a positive influence on both the internal and external corporate image—if there is a company-wide policy concerning standards for computer-generated graphics.

The use of color for business graphics raises problems and opportunities because of the subjective nature of color and the varied emotional responses it evokes. Most people want color graphics because of their aesthetic qualities. However, when graphics are used to communicate quantitative, as opposed to qualitative data, the potential for differences in perception and psychological reaction by different individuals shown the same set of colors suggests that great care must be exercised in their use. Some individuals advise against the use of color for financial data.

Color has a unique ability to capture and focus the attention of a viewer and can add emphasis to a set of data. Properly used, color is of significant value. It is most effective when used with restraint, so that the colors themselves are not the dominant element of a graphic display but rather are used to differentiate between displays of different subjects.

How to Get Started with Business Graphics

Computer graphics in a business is a means and not an end in itself. Unless it is cost justifiable and can increase the profitability of a firm, it has no business being there. The computer graphics industry offers many products and services, but unfortunately, there are very few guidelines for measuring the benefits of a computer graphic application. Those suggested by individuals such as Alan Paller, President of AUI Data Graphics, require dollar value estimates of time savings by managers and analysts as well as estimated value of better presentations related to sales, project management, and overall executive decision making. Estimated annual savings are compared to estimated costs for a computer graphic system, whose cost is amortized over a number of years. This comparative analysis is a means for justifying the expenditure as an investment whose costs will produce a benefit equal to or greater than the corporate return on assets criteria for major expenditures. Paller points out, however, that in many cases computer graphic capabilities are acquired by a large corporation merely because a senior executive decides he "wants it."

Before attempting to evaluate a specific computer graphics system or service, one must identify its specific applications. An application may involve use of computers to support an existing activity such as the preparation of presentation graphics. Other applications, such as the use of computer mapping for market research or the graphic display of financial statements, are often totally new to an organization. Organizations which are exploring new applications may benefit from the initial assistance of a consultant.

A conservative and deliberate approach to getting started with computer graphics would include learning from the experience of others, trying (using) computer graphics before making a capital investment, and being aware of the rapid changes taking place in the options available for hardware, software, and services. Information concerning costs and benefits of a computer graphics application can be obtained from talking with others who have been involved with similar applications. Such information can frequently be obtained at conferences, seminars, or through referrals from computer vendors.

Business graphics involve the use of a new communication medium and, as such, can benefit from the development of an in-house user training program. The initial trainees and system users should preferably have a background or interest in the visual arts (photography, painting, and so on).

Computer Graphics Services

To eliminate or postpone the capital equipment expenditure, one can purchase computer-generated graphic products prepared by a computer graphics service company. Valuable experience can be gained from the specification and use of such graphics. Subsequent demand for more graphics may justify capital investment in a computer graphics system, to bring the capability in-house. There are a growing number of computer graphics services available, some of which are specifically designed to provide a graphic product for walk-in customers.

Walk-in computer graphics service centers usually have trained personnel to assist in the selection of a computer graphic format for a particular application. In some cases, the customer is offered a standard chart book from which to select a format, then the data are entered on a keyboard, and the final graphic product produced as a pen plotter drawing, color xerox print, 35 mm slide, 8x10 Polaroid print, or a Polaroid overhead transparency. Such a service may become common at copy centers, graphic art supply stores, and print shops. One drawback of a walk-in center is that the amount of data that can be displayed is limited to what can be typed in at a keyboard.

Professional service organizations that provide specialized applications assistance are another option. Their added value includes expertise in a specific applications area such as demographic or economic analysis, market research, or accounting. As a result, they can often provide solutions as well as necessary tools. In addition, they are likely to have larger computing resources (hardware), a variety of graphic, statistical and data base management software, plus access to a variety of data bases from public and private sources. Such an organization can help a customer develop an application, and can design a specific turnkey package of hardware and software and assist in its future use and enhancement.

Computer Graphics Time-Sharing

Computer time-sharing companies allow a user to have in-house graphics capability with only a minimal capital investment. CRT terminals can be installed at the user's site and connected by telephone to an external computer time-sharing service that provides access to a computer, a variety of software packages, and specialized data bases. Customer assistance is also available in the operation and sometimes in the application of a computer graphics software package. Hard copy may be provided through a printer or plotter at the user's site or at the computer time-sharing office. In some cases, specialized graphic hard copy devices (for example, a large plotter or a camera) may be accessed in this way. One drawback of this approach is that the telecommunications cost may be quite high due to the volume of data that must be transmitted to send a graphic image to a CRT display or a hardcopy device at the user's site.

Desk Top Graphics

The newer desk top terminals increasingly can display words, numbers, and graphics. The terminal screens vary in the quality of their resolution (apparent smoothness of a curved or diagonal line) but nearly all newer terminals can be used to create some form of graphic display. Graphics may be sent to the terminal for display from a remote computer or may be created at the terminal itself.

Graphic displays produced and transmitted from a remote computer require high-speed telecommunications. In most cases, the need for high-speed lines will limit the distance between the host computer and a graphics terminal to a few thousand feet.

Graphic displays can be produced solely by the desk top computer if the device contains a microprocessor allowing it to function as an "intelligent" terminal. Such devices can communicate with other intelligent terminals as well as with large computers. In addition, large computers can be used to store and transmit data to the terminal which then performs the graphic drawing operations using its own microprocessor.

A low cost printing device attached to a desk top computer can produce a paper copy of the image on a CRT screen. Usually, the resulting print has lower resolution than the screen image and is in black and white. Many microcomputers offer color displays, but to obtain color hard copy you must have specialized equipment. Higher resolution color hard copy can be produced by transmitting the data to another location where more specialized graphic output devices are available for multiple users. An advantage of the intelligent desk top computer is that it permits you to preview an image (or many alternative images) locally, without having to buy a large computer or a specialized, hardcopy graphic output device. In addition to providing screen images, the desk top graphic terminal will often have magnetic disc storage available. A copy of any image can be stored electronically and later accessed from disc, as conveniently as slides are stored and then accessed via a projector.

Adding Graphics to an In-House Computer

Often, a company's existing computers can be used to produce graphics by the addition of software plus graphic display devices. Computer graphics software may be acquired from a computer manufacturer, a graphic terminal manufacturer, or a software company. We do not recommend having graphics software written by in-house computer programmers. It is more economical to lease or buy commercially available software than to create, document, and maintain your own. All software is designed to operate only on specific computers, and thus one's choice will be limited to software compatible with hardware already on hand. The wide range of capabilities offered by different vendors can only be evaluated in the context of each particular application.

Definition of an application and specification of its requirements are needed before computer graphics software packages are evaluated. The specifications will also serve to determine graphic display equipment (hardware) needs. Telecommunications requirements should be considered if a host computer is to operate with remote graphic terminals. Finally, three types of human resources are required: 1) technical assistance for support of specialized graphic hardware, software, and data bases, 2) graphic design consultation for establishing graphic formats and standards, and 3) applications assistance concerning user needs, training, and feedback.

Data driven applications are particularly well suited to the addition of graphics software on an existing computer. When simple graphics are added to recurring reports, the same computer printing hardware can be used to produce both the tabular and graphic results.

Adding a Computer to In-House Graphics

Computers may be used in an in-house graphic arts department to automate some of its manual operations, thus increasing staff productivity and creativity. Graphic arts departments can use a computer to help refine and manipulate electronic images. A computer can create finished art work from initial sketches or roughs. The more expensive devices offer a wide choice of fonts, color, symbols and formats as well as sophisticated techniques to aid composition and reproduction using a wide range of print materials.

Initial applications for business graphics would include automation of existing procedures for producing presentation graphics. As analysts and managers within a corporation begin to use word and data processing desk top terminals that can also produce low resolution graphic displays, a graphic arts department may find itself increasingly being asked to produce presentation quality graphics from the low resolution graphics originally produced by others. Specialized equipment for creating high resolution graphics could then be located within the graphic arts department. That department should have a primary involvement in the development of an organization's graphic standards to ensure effective graphic communication.

Future Uses of Computer Graphics

Computer graphics offers entirely new opportunities for acquiring and interpreting information. These new opportunities result from the ability of graphics to serve as a language for visually describing patterns within a set of data. The observed patterns illustrate relationships that have been "captured" by the data but which normally are not apparent when the data are in their original form or in summary tabular format. Government officials, educators, the average citizen, and business managers, can all expect to be affected by the impact of computer graphics.

Business Graphics

In business, graphics will become a standard part of the management reports used for performance monitoring, analytical studies, and decision support. Recurring, data driven reports will include graphic summaries produced by "graphic report generators." Specialized, idea-driven studies such as those done by market research and financial analysts increasingly will use interactive graphics, which allow for evaluation of what if, where if, and when if, questions. Project planning, mathematical modeling, and developmental training programs also will be major applications for interactive computer graphics.

Graphic decision-support systems will provide senior managers and executives with recurring reports concerning performance within each division of a corporation as well as the corporation's performance within its markets. Financial reports and evaluations of alternative capital investments will use graphics for analytical as well as presentation purposes.

Management and analyst work stations will produce graphic displays and there will be a trend away from the use of keyboards and toward touch-and voice-activated graphics. Senior management and executives will have most graphics prepared for them on paper or on projection screens that can display information available from a graphic data base.

Graphic data bases, graphic data base management software, and wide bandwidth telecommunication networks will provide access to large quantities of highly diverse and rapidly comprehensible information. Commercial graphic data base vendors will provide information for evaluating problems and opportunities such as those involving location, which are beyond the scope of traditional numerical analysis.

New sources of information, such as that provided by NASA's Landsat satellite, will provide opportunities for energy exploration and natural resource management. Figure 4 illustrates how the St. Regis Paper Company was able to identify changes which had taken place in the distribution of its hardwood and softwood by overlaying data obtained from Landsat with field survey data compiled several years earlier.

Graphic standards will become a critical element in the development of descriptive and analytic graphic languages. Development of business graphic applications may precede those within government because of their clearer function and the availability of financial resources, but both will benefit from the results of academic research regarding graphic languages.

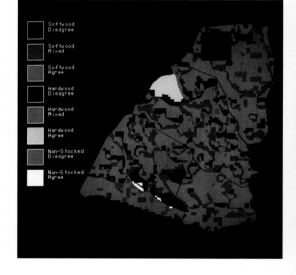

4

PERCEPTION IMPROVED
TO CITYWIDE STANDARD

PERCEPTION REMAINS
HIGHLY NEGATIVE

5

Government Graphics

Federal, state, and local government use of computer graphics will provide greater access to information concerning public needs and government performance. Figure 5, produced by ABT Computer Graphics Corporation, illustrates how computer graphics have been used to assess changes in citizen perception of public service delivery in the City of Boston.

A national census of land will be developed based upon data obtained from satellites, spacecraft and aircraft. Eventually, a national land register will be established to support a multi-purpose land information system. Such a system will provide information needed to rationally manage our nation's most valuable natural resource, our land.

Within cities, urban land information systems can identify not only land and its use but also public and private improvements above and below ground. Such information provides savings and greater efficiency in the construction, maintenance and operation of utility systems. Local land information systems also provide greater accuracy and equity in land taxation programs.

Education Graphics

Computer graphics will provide new opportunities for teaching and research at all levels, from elementary schools through universities. During the last decade, use of hand calculators and microcomputers has begun to permit students to understand ecological, economic, and social processes by use of mathematical models and gaming simulations. Teaching students to understand a process by observing its response to alternative input data goes beyond earlier educational objectives of definition, proof, and construction. Computers have permitted the manipulation of large amounts of data describing complex processes, but the addition of graphics to analyze the interaction of quantitative and qualitative relationships is only beginning. Computer graphics should permit the study of phenomena at many different spatial scales, including microscopic, terrestial, and celestial. Similarly, processes with various temporal scales or rates of change can best be described graphically.

The greatest educational challenge will come from the development of procedures for organizing and manipulating information with a high degree of scale independence. The resulting graphic images will permit the observation of patterns that otherwise would go undetected. This is analogous to the use of a zoom lens on a variable speed motion picture camera to study growth patterns. Such images can describe patterns of change in a process or in any of its constituent parts, including changes in their relationship to one another over time.

Home Graphics

Technology has begun to offer access to information at home via two-way cable television and through the use of personal computers communicating over telephone lines with information vendors. Information services such as The Source provide news wire, stock exchange, weather, travel service, shop at home, bank at home, and what is likely to be an endless stream of information services and products. Public and private data bases will undoubtedly be encyclopedic sources of textual, numeric, and graphic information on any topic imaginable—historic, current, or futuristic. Eventually, such information will probably be available along a continuous scale of subject detail, time, and space aggregation, and will allow a variable perspective zoom on reality (past, present and imagined) for at home education and entertainment. Such a capability might well be known as "map-a-vision."

Miniature "mobile-map" devices will provide a continuously variable graphic representation of one's location when one is travelling, whether by foot or vehicle. The display will offer variable scale and user selectable reference information (for example, roads, topography, structures, and so on).

Recent and projected uses of computer graphics in business indicate that visualization of patterns inherent in data allow for rapid detection, interpretation, and communication of information. If the proverbial equating of information with power, and of time with money, is true, then computer-aided business graphics represent a significant resource for those organizations that choose to use it.

Polaroid Instant Photography in the Computer Graphics Camera

VERNON GORTER

The rapid spread of computer graphics technology in the recent past has been accompanied by a demand for photographic records of the images that are generated and displayed. Polaroid Land films can satisfy the frequent requirement for a hard copy or transparency that is available for virtually instant viewing.

In the 8 x 10 format, Polaroid provides the new Colorgraph film, Type 891, for overhead projection, as well as the Polacolor ER and Polacolor 2 color print films. Many computer graphics cameras can be adapted to also accept Polaroid Land films in the 4 x 5 format, the 3¼ x 4¼ inch pack film format, as well as SX-70 films.

The computer graphics terminal and the computer graphics camera each have a video display. The camera display is designed to interact with photographic film, while the display on the terminal is intended for viewing. Both show the same image, but in a different manner and for very different purposes.

On the following pages we will explain why a special camera display provides the best possible photographic quality, and how you can use the features of the camera to best effect.

The following manufacturers currently make computer graphics cameras: Dunn Instruments, Inc., Image Resource Corporation, and Matrix Instruments, Inc. Some cameras are available in several different models. Also, other manufacturers are known to be planning similar products.

Some camera adjustments must be made by the manufacturer; others you can make yourself. Some of the adjustments you can make yourself will vary somewhat from camera model to camera model.

We will describe here the basic principles of the computer graphics camera and its operation, and show how it fulfills the key requirements for the production of a recorded image of truly high quality.

Why a Computer Graphics Camera?

The video display on a computer graphics terminal is similar to a regular color television screen. It is well known that, with care, the image on a TV screen can be photographed. In fact, if economy is a major consideration and if films of format smaller than 8 x 10 are to be used, you can photograph the video display of the terminal. For a photographic record of higher quality, however, you need a separate camera system.

If we examine the basic disadvantages and limitations of the normal television image, and consider how the computer graphics camera system is designed to greatly reduce these limitations, it will illustrate that a second TV screen, inside the camera system, may be well worth having.

Flatness of image field

The surface of the normal TV screen is designed to have a slight curvature. Camera lenses are generally designed to record sharply a field that is flat. Thus, a photographic record made from a TV screen tends to offer less than optimum overall image sharpness. Also, the screen curvature tends to cause straight lines near the edges of the screen to appear slightly curved.

The video display in the computer graphics camera generally has a relatively flat field, ensuring overall image sharpness as well as freedom from image distortion.

(The computer graphics camera need never be focused by the user. Sharp focus is set automatically for the film format you are using.)

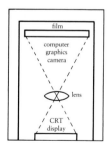 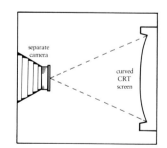

Color homogeneity

The colors in a TV screen image are not homogeneous, but additive—all the infinite hues in an image being made up of appropriate mixtures of minute luminous dots in the primary colors of red, green and blue.

In a color photograph, this dot pattern would tend to desaturate, or reduce the brilliance, of the colors, because there is always a large amount of black present in the image. For example, yellow would be composed of red and green only, the blue dots being black. If red were recorded, both the green and blue dots would appear black.

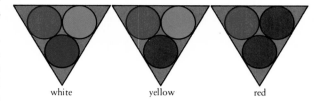

white   yellow   red

In a computer graphics camera this problem is overcome in an ingenious and very effective way.

A black and white display is used. The colors are still added to each other—red and green and blue—but they are not placed next to each other. The colors are added to each other in superimposition. This process is described under **The Three-Exposure Principle**, on page 111. It will be clear from the sketches below that colors of greater brilliance and saturation can be expected.

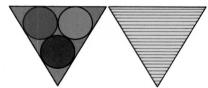

This yellow image area becomes . . . . like this,

and this blue image area becomes . . . . . . like this,

Screen image and color film compatibility

The red, green, and blue color dot pattern in the standard TV image—and in the video display of the computer graphics terminal—is provided by special color phosphors. Unfortunately, the three phosphor colors are by no means totally compatible with the three (red-, green-, and blue-sensitive) layers of photographic color film.

Ideally, the spectral characteristics of each of the three primary colors used to generate the

III

Spectral Characteristics

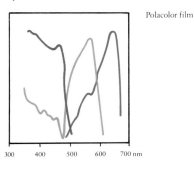

Polacolor film

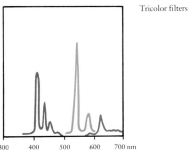

Tricolor filters

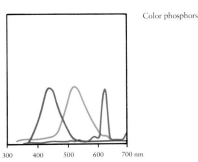

Color phosphors

image should be such as to excite only the corresponding color layer in the film. Red, green, and blue photographic color separation (or tri-color) filters, used in conjunction with a black and white display in the computer graphics camera, meet this requirement much more closely than do the color phosphors.

Image controls

While the computer graphics terminal has only an overall brightness control, the computer graphics camera offers individual controls for each of the three primary colors. Some camera models offer three brightness and contrast controls, while others provide only the three contrast controls. These controls enable the camera to be fine-tuned for very subtle changes, not only in general brightness and contrast, but also in color balance.

Image contrast

The tonal range of a video image that has been adjusted for best viewing quality is generally too wide to be recorded successfully on color film. In most situations, the image that photographs best will look somewhat soft, flat and lifeless on a viewing screen.

By having two video displays—one for viewing and the other for photography—you can get excellent photographic quality without having to sacrifice visual quality, or without having to constantly change the image settings.

The Three-Exposure Principle

The "color separation" process is well known in the printing industry. It is an essential step in full-color printing, enabling virtually all the colors in the orginal art to be reproduced with remarkable accuracy, using inks of just three basic colors (in addition to a black ink).

The colors in the original are "separated" into their three primary components—red, green, and blue. This is done by photographing the original successively through a red, a green, and a blue tricolor or color separation filter. The resultant separation films are used to make three printing plates. The original colors are regenerated on the printer's paper by successively printing from these three plates, in precise register with each other, using three inks of appropriate colors.

The color separation principle is used in the computer graphics camera. When the color film has been loaded into the camera and the dark slide of the film holder has been withdrawn, the shutter button is pressed just once. This sets in motion the following sequence of events:

1 The red component of the image in the color graphics terminal is directed to the black and white CRT screen in the camera. At the same time, a deep red filter (such as a Wratten No. 25) is automatically brought before the camera lens. The film is automatically exposed for a predetermined length of time. The red component of the computer graphics image is thus recorded on the film. The image is not in the form of many minute red dots; it is in the form of a continuous horizontal line pattern, such as is normally associated with a black and white TV image.

The brightness of the red at any specific image point will correspond to the brightness of the red content of the original full-color image at that point.

2 Now, only the green component of the color graphics image is directed to the black and white camera display tube. At the same time, a deep green filter (such as a Wratten No. 58) is automatically placed before the camera lens. The film is once more exposed automatically for a predetermined length of time. The green component of the computer graphics image is now added to the red component on the film.

3 Finally, only the blue component of the color graphics image is brought to the black and white CRT of the camera. A deep blue filter (such as a Wratten No. 47B) is automatically positioned before the camera lens. The film is exposed automatically for a third time, and the blue image component joins the green and red components on the film.

The film is now processed in the normal manner. The result is a brilliant photographic rendition of the original image.

A very important feature of this system is the recording of all three primary-color images on the same CRT line pattern, in superimposition on each other. Thus, for example, yellow is always a homogeneous yellow, and not a combination of a separate green and red.

The diagram (left) shows what happens when the red, green, and blue color components of the original display are separately presented on the black and white CRT screen, photographed through the appropriate tri-color filters, and re-created in the processed color photograph.

In order to keep the example simple, the subject colors have here been limited to black, red, blue, yellow, and white. The principle applies equally to the full range of possible colors. Magenta, for example, would result from a red plus a blue exposure.

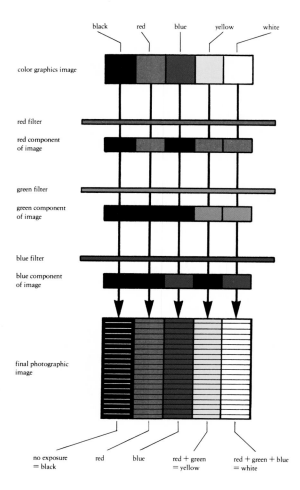

color graphics image

red filter

red component of image

green filter

green component of image

blue filter

blue component of image

final photographic image

black   red   blue   yellow   white

no exposure = black   red   blue   red + green = yellow   red + green + blue = white

What Constitutes a Good Photographic Image?

Before we discuss the various adjustments that can be made in a computer graphics camera, we must define the conditions that are necessary for the production of a color hard copy or transparency of good quality. They are:

1 White areas in the video display must reproduce as nearly white.
2 Black areas in the video display must reproduce as nearly black.

The image brightness range—or contrast—presented by the camera CRT must lie within the limits acceptable to the film being used. If the screen image is too contrasty for the film, image detail will be lost at the bright end or the dark end of the scale, or perhaps at both. If the screen image is too soft, the photographic record will lack good blacks and whites, and will look flat and lifeless.

3 Neutral gray areas in the video display must record as neutral gray in the photographed image, without any color bias.

When gray reproduces as gray, the system is generally set for satisfactory color rendition with the average kind of display, over the normally encountered color range. Good gray, therefore, generally indicates good overall color balance.

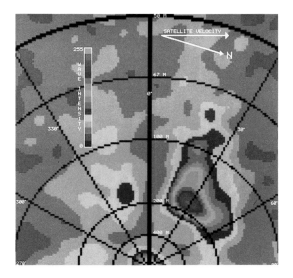

Study of an ocean swell, computed from a satellite image of the Atlantic Ocean near the Florida coast. The 180-meter swell was propagating in a westerly direction from the magenta-purple center near the lower right corner of the photograph. Sixteen colors are used to represent wave intensity, with two white arrows indicating north and the satellite's direction of travel. Photographed on Polaroid Polacolor ER 8 x 10 Land Film, Type 809, in the Image Processing and Computer Graphics Laboratory of the Applied Physics Laboratory, Johns Hopkins University, Laurel, Maryland.

The Camera Controls

The controls of the computer graphics camera will have been set by the supplier of the camera, for use with your specific computer graphics terminal and with the Polaroid Land film you have indicated you will be using.

In theory, the controls should not require subsequent adjustment, except in the rare event that you should change to a different computer graphics terminal, or the more likely event that you might want to use a different film type.

In practice, you may find that adjustments of the camera settings are called for in order to compensate for variables such as a slight change in the characteristics of the film over a period of time, or progressive electronic drift in the system, or to suit the specific characteristics of a series of computer images that are to be photographed.

The camera controls, and their manner of operation, vary from camera model to camera model. Some controls you will be able to adjust yourself, while others may require adjustment by the supplier of the camera. Thus, the information that follows is of a general nature, designed to provide the greatest possible help to all users. For details relating to a specific camera model, consult the supplier of the camera.

All cameras have controls for *exposure time* and *image contrast*; some cameras also have *image brightness* controls. A camera has three controls in each of the above categories—for each of the red, green, and blue color components of the image.

The only color filters that are used in the computer graphics camera are the three built-in tricolor filters. Fine-tuning of color balance is never achieved with the use of additional filters, but only with the camera controls mentioned above.

Exposure time control

This control, as its name indicates, serves to regulate the length of time for which the film is exposed to the video image in the camera.

In some camera models the exposure times are pre-set by the manufacturer of the camera and can only be adjusted by the camera manufacturer or supplier; in other cameras the exposure times can be adjusted by the user.

Depending on the camera model used, the exposure time control may, or may not, provide the most convenient and effective way to adjust color balance. (Ask your camera supplier for details.) The relationship between the red, green, and blue exposures must be such that the color balance in the photograph image is as desired.

It is important to realize that the three exposure times differ greatly in length. Typically, the red exposure might be 50 seconds, the green exposure 6 seconds, and the blue exposure 2 seconds. Thus, any adjustment in exposure times must be proportional, rather than purely in terms of seconds. For example, to reduce the red content of a hard copy or transparency by about 50 percent, you could either halve the red exposure (from 50 to 25 seconds), or you could double both the green and blue exposures (from 6 to 12 seconds and from 2 to 4 seconds, respectively).

While both of the above methods would have virtually the same effect on the color balance, the first would have the additional effect of darkening the image somewhat, while the second would cause the image to become considerably lighter. (See also **The Color Test Chart**, page 115.)

Brightness and contrast controls

These controls are presented under one heading, because they normally need to be used in conjunction with each other. Used individually, the contrast control acts to increase or decrease the luminance difference between the lightest and darkest image parts, while the brightness control changes the luminance of the image uniformly over its tonal range.

When user-adjustment of the exposure times is not possible or desirable, the color balance can be fine-tuned by the use of the brightness and contrast controls instead. If the camera does not have brightness controls, color balance can generally be adjusted quite satisfactorily using the contrast controls only.

White level and black level adjustment

The brightness range of each of the three images that appear, successively, on the screen of the computer graphics camera can be changed from the settings provided by the camera supplier by adjusting the white and black levels of those images.

The overall color balance of the photographed image can be changed by raising or lowering the white level of one of the colors in relationship to the other two colors. (To maintain the desired image brightness range, the black level may need to be readjusted accordingly.)

Unfortunately, there is no single control knob which enables you to set the white (maximum luminance) and black (minimum luminance) levels on your camera video screen. To make these screen luminance adjustments, you must use the brightness and contrast controls together.

While the brightness control will shift the whole tonal scale up or down, the contrast control is designed to have a predominant effect on either the white level or the black level selectively, with little or no effect on the other level. Normally, the proper setting of the white and black levels will require you to go back and forth a few times between brightness and contrast control, to achieve the desired values.

If your camera does not have brightness controls, you must use the contrast control to raise or lower the white level. This will, however, also cause the image brightness range (contrast) to change somewhat.

Most camera models incorporate a movable photometer, which enables you to accurately read the camera screen luminances.

To make the white level settings in the camera, you must first set the computer graphics terminal screen to maximum white. To make the black level settings, first set the computer graphics terminal screen to maximum black. For the greatest possible accuracy, it is desirable to set the entire screen to white or black, and to make the photometer readings from a central part of the camera screen.

On most camera models, each of the brightness and contrast control knobs has some kind of engraved scale. Be sure to make a note of the setting of each control before making adjustments, so that you can easily return to the original settings.

The chart below gives some indication of what constitutes an acceptable white level to black level ratio (or image brightness range) on the camera screen, as read by the photometer.

Nature of Display	Polaroid Land Film	Recommended Brightness Range
"Graphic" displays	Colorgraph Type 891	about 200:1
	Polacolor ER	about 200:1
	Polacolor 2	about 100:1
	SX-70	about 150:1
Displays of a "pictorial" nature	Colorgraph Type 891	about 80:1
	Polacolor ER	about 80:1
	Polacolor 2	about 40:1
	SX-70	about 60:1

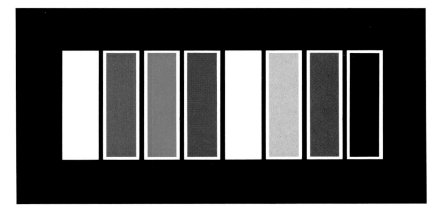

The Test Photograph

Before you begin using a computer graphics camera for routine work, make a test photograph and evaluate it carefully. If the computer graphics test image has not been reproduced satisfactorily, make the required camera adjustments or, if necessary, have the camera supplier make them.

If, at any time, you decide to adjust the camera controls yourself, for any of the reasons indicated in the earlier sections of this article, make a test photograph and evaluate it carefully, before you go on to routine work with your camera.

Put into the computer graphics system a test image which has the following characteristics:

1 An area of white.
2 An area of black.
3 An area of neutral gray of a density similar to the gray along the left border of the test chart on page 116.
4 At least three key colors, such as blue, green, and red.

Expose the film to the test image, process the film, and evaluate the photograph.

White areas in the computer graphics test image should reproduce as very nearly white. Black areas should reproduce as black. If the test image contains two levels of gray, the difference in their densities should be clearly visible in the photographed image.

If black is not black (but too light), reduce the black luminance levels. If white is not white (but grayish and muddy), raise the white levels or, if you can do so, increase the exposure times. (If you increase the exposure times to achieve white, you may need to readjust the black levels, to maintain black.)

To correct a color imbalance in your hard copy or transparency, use the test chart, described below.

The Color Test Chart

A color photograph may have an overall color imbalance, causing the entire image to appear to have a distinct veil of one color superimposed on it. While such a color excess is generally clearly detectable from the total image, it is most easily evaluated—to establish its exact color and magnitude—in a neutral gray image area.

To determine the nature of a color imbalance, and the corrective action needed to remove it in a subsequent photo, compare the neutral gray area in your test print or transparency with the color strip along the left edge of your test chart. (When you compare a color transparency with the test chart, it is important to view the transparency by the illumination in which it will normally be seen—the projection light. As far as is possible, a color print should also be evaluated by illumination under which it is expected to be normally viewed.)

If there is no color imbalance, the gray in the photo will resemble the neutral gray that surrounds the color patches on the chart.

If the gray in the photo looks blue (as in the top color patch), there is a blue color imbalance; if the gray in the photo appears reddish, there is a red imbalance.

In making your evaluations, remember that yellow is a mixture of green and red, magenta is a mixture of blue and red, and cyan is a mixture of blue and green.

How to read the chart

—   means decrease exposure
+   means increase exposure
R = Red
G = Green
B = Blue
C = Cyan
M = Magenta
Y = Yellow

For example, —B 30% means that you should reduce the exposure for blue by about 30 percent; —G 15% +B 20% +R 20% means that you should reduce the exposure for green by about 15 percent and increase the exposure for blue and red by about 20 percent each.

The exposure adjustments can be made by changing the exposure times or by altering the screen luminances (white level and black level settings).

How to determine and make the color correction

1 To establish the hue, or color, of an imbalance, determine which of the six color patches matches most closely the gray area in your photo.
2 Having determined the color of the imbalance, estimate the magnitude of that imbalance.

   If the magnitude of the imbalance matches the color patch in the chart, use the values indicated in the chart.

If the imbalance is significantly greater than the color in the patch, double all the values in the chart.

If the imbalance is just barely noticeable, halve all the values in the chart.

3 Examine the overall tonal density of the photo.

   If, in addition to having a color imbalance, the photographic image appears too light, follow the left column in the chart.

   If, in addition to having a color imbalance, the image appears too dark, follow the center column.

   If the image only has a color imbalance, but is satisfactory in overall density, follow the right column.

   If your test photo has no color imbalance, but is either too light or too dark, adjust all three exposure values by the same proportion.

4 Make another test photo, using the recommended corrections. Repeat the evaluation and correction process, if necessary.

If gray area appears	and image is too light	and image is too dark	and image has correct overall tonal density
too red	− R 30%	+ B 35% + G 35%	− R 15% + B 20% + G 20%
too green	− G 30%	+ B 35% + R 35%	− G 15% + B 20% + R 20%
too blue	− B 30%	+ B 35% + R 35%	− B 15% + G 20% + R 20%
too cyan (blue and green)	− B 25% − G 25%	+ R 40%	+ R 20% − B 15% − G 15%
too magenta (blue and red)	− B 25% − R 25%	+ G 40%	+ G 20% − B 15% − R 15%
too yellow (green and red)	− G 25% − R 25%	+ B 40%	+ B 20% − G 15% − R 15%

This chart is intended as a useful guide, and is not an infallible color correction indicator.

Variable factors, such as the reciprocity effect of the film under a wide variety of circumstances, and the exact overall image brightness of the first test picture, render precise recommendations impossible.

Glossary

Achromatic color. One that is found along the gray scale from white to black.

Additive primaries. See **Primary colors.**

Algorithm. Procedure, typically composed of mathematical functions, for performing a task, such as removing hidden lines from the display of a three-dimensional solid object.

Aliasing. Undesirable visual effects (sometimes called artifacts) in computer-generated images, caused by improper sampling techniques. The most common effect is a jagged edge along object boundaries.

Alphanumeric. Letters of the alphabet, numerals or symbols.

Anti-aliasing. A filtering technique to give the appearance of smooth lines and edges in a raster image. The technique involves use of intermediate intensities between neighboring pixels to soften the "stairstep effect" of sloped lines.

Application. Task to be performed by a computer program or system. Broad examples of computer graphics applications are mapping, engineering design and drafting, business chart making, and facilities management.

Array. Data structure which stores the memory location of points by coordinates. A two-dimensional array stores x,y coordinates. A three-dimensional array stores x,y,z coordinates allowing for depth representation.

Boolean. Pertaining to the symbolic logic system developed by British mathematician George Boole.

Business graphics. Bar charts, pie charts, graphs and other visual representations of the operational or strategic aspects of a business, such as market share, sales vs. costs, comparative product performance, etc. Also called management graphics as they are intended to aid management in assimilating and presenting business data.

Calligraphic. See **Vector.**

Cartographic data base (CDB). Data base which contains in digital form the x,y coordinates defining a geographic area. Combined with an attribute file (containing values for a spatially distributed variable), a CDB can produce a computer map of the distribution of a variable in a region.

Cathode ray tube (CRT). A type of graphic display which produces an image by directing a beam of electrons to activate a phosphor-coated surface in a vacuum tube. The CRT is the most common type of monitor used in interactive graphics systems.

Central processing unit (CPU). Main frame, or, more specifically, the central processor of a computer system, containing the arithmetic unit and logic. (In a microcomputer, the CPU is often on a single chip called a microprocessor.)

Chroma. See **Saturation.**

Chromaticity. Dominant wavelength and purity of a color as objectively measured; corresponds to hue and saturation of the color without regard to brightness.

CIE diagram. A diagram developed in 1931 by the Commission Internationale de l'Eclairage (International Commission on Illumination) to show the entire gamut of perceivable colors, expressed in chromaticity coordinates derived from tristimulus values of the spectrum under standardized viewing conditions.

Clipping. The process of removing portions of an image which are outside the boundaries of the display screen.

Coherence. Assumption used in raster scan technology which attributes the same value of an individual pixel to its adjacent pixel.

Color map. A table storing the definitions of the red, green and blue components of colors to be displayed.

Color solid. See **Color space.**

Color space. The type of three-dimensional coordinate system that defines a model showing colors organized in space by attributes such as hue, lightness and saturation. A physical model of a color space is called a color solid.

Complementary colors. In an additive system (light), complementary colors combine to produce white light. Each spectral hue is the complement of the mixture of all the other spectral hues. In a subtractive system (pigment or other colorant), complements are opposite each other on the hue circle, and combine to produce a neutral gray.

Concatenate. To link together in a chain. For example, the joining of one line of a display with the succeeding line.

Coordinates. An ordered set of absolute or relative data values which specify a location in a Cartesian coordinate system.

Data base management system (DBMS). A program which enables a data base to be organized to expedite the sorting, updating, extracting or retrieving of information and the generation of reports or desired output.

Data reduction. Extracting needed information from, or organizing into useful form, masses of raw data.

Digital-to-analog converter (DAC). Interface to convert digital data (represented in discrete, discontinuous form) into analog data (represented in continuous form).

Digitizer. Vector graphic input device which can be used to scan an existing image, capturing x,y coordinates at desired intervals.

Direct view storage tube (DVST). Type of graphic display device in which the display does not need to be refreshed, because low level electron flood guns sustain the illuminaton of the phosphors activated by the directed beam.

Disk. Magnetic storage medium on which information can be accessed at random (as opposed to sequentially). Floppy disks are small, portable storage vehicles; hard disks can store much more data. Contrast with **Magnetic tape.**

Filtering. Use of a weighting function to interpolate the value of a pixel from the polygons intersecting it. Filtering techniques are used to solve aliasing problems.

Font. Also called type font. Complete set of all the characters and symbols that make up one size of a typeface.

Frame buffer. Memory device which stores the contents of an image pixel by pixel. Frame buffers are used to refresh a raster image. Sometimes they incorporate local processing ability, and can be used to update the memory. The "depth" of the frame buffer is the number of bits per pixel, which determines the number of colors or intensities which can be displayed.

Gamut. Total range of colors which can be displayed on a monitor.

Gaussian. A Gaussian distribution is a frequency distribution for a set of variable data, sometimes called a normal distribution and typically represented by a bell-shaped curve that is symmetrical about the mean.

Graded series. A scale of colors used in graphics to present change in a variable. A graded series may be composed of progressive change in either lightness or saturation of one hue, in hue steps around the hue circle, or along the gray scale.

Graphic display device. A display terminal or monitor used to display data in a graphic form. The most common types of graphic displays are direct view storage tubes (DVST), raster refresh devices and vector (sometimes called calligraphic or stroke-writing) refresh devices.

Graphic input device. Device such as a digitizer which gives the computer the points which make up an image in such a way that the image can be stored, reconstructed, displayed or manipulated.

Graphic output device. Device used to display or record an image. A display screen is an output device for "soft copy;" hard copy output devices produce paper, film or transparencies of the image.

Hard copy. Tangible copy of an image stored in the computer. Hard copy output devices can produce paper copies, slides, prints, transparencies, pen plots, etc.

Host computer. The central processing unit (CPU) which provides the computing power for terminals and peripheral devices that are connected to it.

Hue. Subjective term which refers to the objectively measurable dominant wavelength of radiant energy on the visible portion of the electromagnetic spectrum; the most basic attribute of color. Used loosely, hue can also refer to mixtures of different wavelengths, such as purple.

Hue circle. A circle formed from the linear spectral hues of violet, blue, green, yellow, orange and red. Intermediary colors of red-violet, blue-violet, blue-green, yellow-green, yellow-orange, and red-orange are often included. Also called a color circle or color wheel.

Incident light. Light falling on an object. The color of an object is perceived as a function of the wavelengths of incident light reflected or absorbed by it.

Intelligent terminal. One with local processing capability. It does not need to be connected to a larger computer to perform certain functions.

Interactive. Immediate response to input. In interactive processing, an image can be modified or edited and the changes seen right away, as contrasted to "batch" processing in which the user must wait for results.

Interlacing. Scanning technique which sends first the even, then the odd lines of a display in the refresh cycle. This reduces flickering effect.

Iterative. Repetitive. Often used when each succeeding "iteration" or repetition of a procedure comes closer to the desired result.

Light pen. Graphic input device which consists of a stylus with a light-detecting mechanism used interactively to give positional information about a display item on a CRT.

Local intelligence. Processing power and memory capacity built in to the terminal so it does not need to be connected to a host computer to perform certain tasks. A "dumb terminal" has no local intelligence.

Look-up table. Table of pixel intensity or color information which increases the range of values that can be displayed. Since the values are stored in the look-up table, they do not have to be computed each time they are called up, and execution time is reduced.

Luminance. Amount of radiant energy per unit area as objectively measurable. The subjective synonym is brightness.

Machine readable. Encoded in digital format.

Magnetic tape. Storage device which can only retrieve information sequentially, i.e. by searching the tape from beginning to end. Contrast with **Disk.**

Matrix printer. Usually called a dot matrix printer because it produces images formed from dots which conform to a matrix unit. For example, a 5 x 7 dot character size is frequently used on low resolution displays.

Metamer. Color which is perceived to be the same as another color even though they have different spectral energy distributions. Metamers may look the same under one lighting condition, and show their difference under another condition.

Microcomputer. A small computer containing a microprocessor, input and display devices, and memory all in one box. It may or may not interface to a host computer and/or peripheral devices. Sometimes referred to as a desk top computer, or a personal computer.

Microprocessor. A single chip or integrated circuit containing the entire central processing unit (CPU).

Moiré pattern. Wavy line distortion of an image which can be caused by sampling error.

Monitor. Display device in an interactive graphics system.

Munsell system. A perceptual color system which identifies color in terms of hue, value and chroma, arranged in orderly scales of equal visual steps. A notation assigning a numerical equivalent to each attribute on its scale yields a unique designation for any given color. Standardized color chips sampling the Munsell color space and labelled by Munsell notation are used internationally to express the perceived color of an object, to match colors, etc.

Mylar. DuPont's trade name for a type of film which may be used in plotters instead of a paper medium because it is stronger and more dimensionally stable, an important consideration for engineering and architectural drawings of high accuracy. Large plots on Mylar or other transparent or translucent media can also be copied at much lower cost.

Persistence. The length of time an image produced on a display device by activated phosphors remains clear, bright and sharp.

Pixel. Picture cell. A pixel is the smallest unit on the grid of the display screen which can be stored, displayed or addressed.

Plotter. A graphic hard copy output device which can use any of a number of technologies to "plot" an image. Pen plotters, electrostatic plotters, photo-plotters, ink-jet plotters and laser plotters are some examples.

Presentation graphics. High quality graphics intended to visually reinforce points made in the presentation of proposals, plans, budgets, etc. to top management.

Primary colors. A set of colors from which all other colors can be derived, but which cannot be produced from each other. The additive primaries (light) are red, green and blue. The subtractive primaries (colorant) are yellow, magenta (a deep pink) and cyan (a blue-green). The psychological primaries (perceived as basic and unmixed) are the pairs red/green, yellow/blue and black/white.

Primitive element. Graphic element such as a point or line segment which can be readily called up and extrapolated or combined with other primitive elements to form more complex objects or images in two or three dimensions.

Pseudo-colors. Also called false colors. Colors arbitrarily assigned to an image to represent data values, rather than natural likeness. Often used in satellite imagery.

Raster. Grid. A raster display device stores and displays data as horizontal rows of uniform grid or picture cells (pixels). Contrast **Vector.**

Real time image generation. Performance of the computations necessary to update the image is completed within the refresh rate, so the sequence appears correctly to the viewer. An example is flight simulation, in which thousands of computations must be performed to present an animated image, all within the 30-60 cycles per second rate at which the frames change.

Reflectance model. Function which describes light on a surface by making assumptions concerning light sources, angles, surface texture, etc. Also called illumination model.

Refresh. Rewriting of an image to the display screen to "refresh" the phosphors and maintain a constant image. Typically the rate the image must be regenerated to avoid flicker is 30 to 60 cycles per second (hertz).

Remote terminal. Computer terminal which is cabled to a larger computer. A remote terminal may or may not have local processing capability.

Report generator. A technique for automatically producing standard reports from an input file and instructions for the format and contents of the desired output file. A "graphic report generator" would be capable of providing a visual summary of routine data the same way tabular reports now provide a statistical summary.

Resolution. Number of pixels per unit of area. A display with a finer grid contains more pixels and thus has a higher resolution, capable of reproducing more detail in an image.

RGB. Red, green, blue; commonly used to refer to the color space, mixing system or monitor in color computer graphics. In RGB, a color is defined as percentages of red, green and blue (the additive primaries).

Routine. Set of instructions to the computer to perform a certain function. For example, an inking routine translates the graphic input from a light pen into visible continuous lines, giving the user the impression of sketching with the stylus.

Sampling rate. Frequency at which points are recorded in digitizing an image. Sampling errors can cause aliasing effects.

Saturation. A subjective term which usually refers to the difference of a hue from a gray of the same value. Colors can be desaturated by adding white, adding black, adding gray, or adding the complementary color. In a subtractive system, adding the complement will make the color darker. In an additive system, adding the complement will make the color lighter. This creates confusion since value, as well as saturation, is changed. **Chroma** is used the same way as saturation, but a distinction is sometimes made that saturation is relative whereas chroma is absolute. Purity is an objective term which denotes a measurement that can be visualized on a chromaticity chart as a position between the equal energy mixture of all colors (white) to the dominant wavelength of the color.

Scanning. Process of reading data in regular horizontal sweeps to cover the entire image or screen. Scan conversion refers to the process of putting data into grid format for display on a raster device.

Scatter plot. Also called scatter diagram or dot chart. Shows a two-variable frequency distribution by plotting a dot or symbol at each data point. Sometimes a line or curve is added to show the correlation (if there is one) between the variables represented on the two axes.

Simultaneous contrast. Changes in the appearance of a color relative to its background or adjacent colors.

Spatial data. Locational data. Usually refers to distribution of a variable or the relationships between variables in a geographic region. Demographic features, marketing distributions, energy resource data and topographic data are examples of information readily represented spatially, i.e. on a map.

Spectral color. Color of a single wavelength on the visible portion of the electromagnetic spectrum. Refraction of white light yields the spectral hues ranging from violet with the shortest wavelength through blue, green, yellow, orange, and ending with red at the longest wavelength. Black, white, and colors which are mixtures of wavelengths are not spectral colors.

Spectral energy distribution. Diagram showing the component wavelengths of a color, as measured by a spectrophotometer.

Subtractive primaries. See **Primary colors.**

Telecommunications. Communication from one computer terminal or system to another via telephone lines.

Timesharing. The sharing of a main computer facility by many users, each of whom has a remote terminal. Processing time is "shared" so the users are unaware of each other.

Trace. Scanning path of the beam in a raster display.

Transformation. Performance of mathematical calculations such as matrix algebra to rotate, scale or otherwise manipulate a graphic image whose coordinates are stored in the computer.

Triangulate. To divide polygons or a set of points into a network of triangles, rather than superimposing a grid structure.

Trichromatic. Three-colored. In computer graphics, trichromatic generally refers to the three primary colors combined to create all others: red, green and blue.

Tristimulus values. Relative amounts of three primary colors that are combined to create a color.

Turnkey system. Computer system containing all the hardware and software needed to perform a given application.

Value. Comparison of a chromatic color to an achromatic color situating it along a gray scale from white to black. Other words used synonymously are brightness, brilliance, intensity, lightness, luminosity and luminance. Sometimes a distinction is made that value is the perceived non-blackness of a color, whereas brightness is the measurable amount of energy in a color. The brightness definition is used when colors must be chosen so as to remain distinguishable on a black and white monitor, whereas value can be used when fully saturated or pure hues are given equal weight. Lightness, the amount of energy present in a color, refers to non-self-luminous objects, while brightness refers to self-luminous objects. Luminosity is a subjective term for the amount of light emitted, transmitted, or reflected. Luminance is an objective term for the amount of radiant energy per unit area.

Vector. Line drawing or "calligraphic." A vector display device stores and displays data as line segments identified by the x,y coordinates of their end points. Contrast **Raster.**

Video display. Television type display (raster format), which uses an analog signal. A digital-to-analog converter transforms the digital information to a video signal that is used for display.

Work station. Configuration of computer equipment designed to be used by one person at a time. A work station may have a terminal connected to a larger computer, or may be a "standalone" with local processing capability. It generally consists of an input device (keyboard, digitizer, etc.), a display device, memory, and an output device such as a printer or plotter.

XYZ space. A three-dimensional coordinate system based on the 1931 CIE chromaticity diagram which plots X, Y, and Z as the tristimulus values of a color.

Selected Bibliography and References

Resource Publications and Organizations

ACM Transactions on Graphics. Association for Computing Machinery, Inc., P.O. Box 12115, Church Street Station, New York, NY 10249; (212) 265-6300. (Quarterly)

The Anderson Report. Anderson Publishing Co., Simi Valley Business Park, P.O. Box 3534, Simi Valley, CA 93063; (805) 581-1184. (Monthly)

Color: Research and Application. John Wiley & Sons, Journal Dept., 605 Third Avenue, New York, NY 10158; (212) 850-6000. (Quarterly)

Computer Graphics "A Quarterly Report of SIG-GRAPH-ACM" (Special Interest Group on Computer Graphics). Association for Computing Machinery, Inc., P.O. Box 12105, Church Street Station, New York, NY 10249; (212) 265-6300.

Computer Graphics and Image Processing "An International Journal." Academic Press, 111 Fifth Avenue, New York, NY 10003; (212) 741-6800. (Monthly)

Computer Graphics for Management. The Management Roundtable, Inc., 824 Boylston Street, Chestnut Hill, MA 02167; (617) 232-8080. (Monthly)

Computer Graphics News. AUI Data Graphics, 1701 K Street N.W., Third Floor, Washington, DC 20006; (202) 331-1800. (Monthly)

Computer Graphics News. Scherago Associates, Inc., 1515 Broadway, New York, NY 10036; (212) 730-1050. (Bimonthly)

Computer Graphics Software News. Greg Passmore, 910 Ashford Parkway, Houston, TX (713) 493-5550. (Biweekly)

Computer Graphics World. Cygnus Publications, Inc., 54 Mint Street, San Francisco, CA 94103; (415) 543-0978. (Monthly) [Monthly column "Computer Business Graphics" started Dec. 1981]

Computers and Graphics. Pergamon Press, Inc., Maxwell House, Fairview Park, Elmsford, NY 10523; (914) 592-7700. (Quarterly)

Harvard Library of Computer Graphics. A 17-volume set of technical papers and case studies on computer graphics hardware, software and applications. Laboratory for Computer Graphics & Spatial Analysis, Harvard University Graduate School of Design, Gund Hall, Cambridge, MA 02138; (617) 495-4004. (Annual conference proceedings)

IEEE Computer Graphics and Applications. IEEE Computer Society, 10662 Los Vaqueros Circle, Los Alamitos, CA 90720; (714) 821-8380. (Bimonthly)

The S. Klein Directory of Computer Graphics Suppliers. Hardware, Software, Systems and Services. S. Klein, 730 Boston Post Road, Suite 27, P.O. Box 392, Sudbury, MA 01776; (617) 443-4671.

The S. Klein Newsletter on Computer Graphics. S. Klein, 730 Boston Post Road, P.O. Box 89, Sudbury, MA 01776; (617) 443-4671. (Biweekly)

National Computer Graphics Association (NCGA), 2033 M Street N.W., Suite 330, Washington, DC 20036; (202) 466-5895. (Annual conference proceedings)

Special Interest Group on Computer Graphics (SIG-GRAPH), Association for Computing Machinery, Inc., 1133 Avenue of the Americas, New York, NY 10036; (212) 265-6300. (Annual conference proceedings)

Computer Graphics—General Bibliography

Angell, I. O. *A Practical Introduction to Computer Graphics.* New York: Halsted Press (A Division of John Wiley & Sons), 1981.

Bliss, F. W. and G. M. Hyman. "Selecting and Implementing a Turnkey Graphics System." *IEEE Computer Graphics and Applications* 1 (April 1981): 55-70.

Bolt, R. *Spatial Data Management.* Cambridge, MA: MIT Architecture Machine Group, 1979.

Bylinsky, G. "A New Industrial Revolution is on the Way." *Fortune* (October 5, 1981): 106-114.

Cakir, A., D. J. Hart and T. F. M. Stewart. *Visual Display Terminals.* New York: John Wiley & Sons, 1980.

Chasen, S. H. *Geometric Principles and Procedures for Computer Graphics Applications.* Englewood Cliffs, NJ: Prentice-Hall, 1978.

Chasen, S. H. and J. W. Dow. *The Guide for the Evaluation and Implementation of CAD/CAM Systems.* Atlanta: CAD/CAM Decisions, 1979.

Conrac Corporation. *Raster Graphics Handbook.* Covina, CA: Conrac Division, Conrac Corporation, 1980.

Demel, J. et al. *Computer Graphics.* College Station, TX: Creative Publishing, 1979.

Foley, J. D. and A. van Dam. *Fundamentals of Interactive Computer Graphics.* Reading, MA: Addison-Wesley, 1981.

Freeman, H., ed. *Tutorial and Selected Readings in Interactive Computer Graphics.* Los Alamitos, CA: IEEE Computer Society, 1980.

Garboden, C. "Computer Graphics." *Close-Up.* Cambridge, MA: Polaroid Corporation, July 1979.

Giloi, W. *Interactive Computer Graphics: Data Structures, Algorithms, Languages.* Englewood Cliffs, NJ: Prentice-Hall, 1978.

Hatfield, L. and B. Herzog. "Graphics Software—From Techniques to Principles." *IEEE Computer Graphics and Applications* 2 (January 1982): 59-80.

Leavitt, R., ed. *Artist and Computer.* New York: Harmony Books, 1976.

Lerner, E. J. "The Computer Graphics Revolution." *IEEE Spectrum* 18 (February 1981): 35-39.

Levitan, E. L. *Electronic Imaging Techniques.* New York: Van Nostrand Reinhold Company, 1977.

Machover, C. *Display Systems: Computer Graphics.* Pittsfield, MA: Optical Publishing Co., 1979.

Mueller, R. E. "Idols of Computer Art." *Creative Computing* 4 (May/June 1978): 100-106.

Newman, W. M. and R. F. Sproull. *Principles of Interactive Computer Graphics.* Second edition. New York: McGraw-Hill, 1979.

Parslow, R. D. et al, eds. *Computer Graphics: Techniques and Applications.* New York: Plenum Press, 1975.

Pavlidis, T. *Algorithms for Graphics and Image Processing.* Maryland: Computer Science Press, 1981.

Pratt, W. K. *Digital Image Processing.* New York: Wiley-Interscience, 1978.

Rogers, D. F. and J. A. Adams. *Mathematical Elements for Computer Graphics.* New York: McGraw-Hill, 1976.

Rosenfeld, A. and A. C. Kak. *Digital Picture Processing.* New York: Academic Press, 1976.

Ryan, D. L. *Computer-Aided Graphics and Design.* New York: Marcel Dekker, 1979.

"Say It With Pictures." *Datamation* 27 (August 1981): 55+.

Scott, J. E. *Introduction to Interactive Computer Graphics.* New York: John Wiley & Sons, 1982.

Sherr, S. *Electronic Displays.* New York: John Wiley & Sons, 1979.

Waite, M. *Computer Graphics Primer.* Indianapolis, IN: Howard W. Sams & Co., Inc., 1979.

Yen, E. H. "A Graphics Glossary." *Computer Graphics* 15 (August 1981).

Business Graphics and Graphic Design

ANSI. *Time Series Charts.* ANSI Standard Y.15.2M. New York: American National Standards Institute, 1979.

ANSI. *Illustrations for Publication and Projection.* ANSI Standard Y.15.1M. New York: American National Standards Institute, 1979.

Berryman, G. *Notes on Graphic Design and Visual Communication.* Los Altos, CA: William Kaufmann, Inc., 1979.

Cardamore, T. *Chart and Graph Preparation Skills.* New York: Van Nostrand Reinhold Company, 1981.

Copithorne, D. "Computer Graphics: Data on Display." *Output* 1 (April 1980): 28-31+.

Dreyfuss, H. *Symbol Sourcebook: An Authoritative Guide to International Graphic Symbols.* New York: McGraw-Hill, 1972.

Enrick, N. L. *Effective Graphic Communication.* Princeton, NJ: Auerbach, 1972.

Hanks, K. and L. Belliston. *Rapid Vis: A New Method for the Rapid Visualization of Ideas.* Los Altos, CA: William Kaufmann, Inc., 1980.

Harvill, L. R. and T. L. Kraft. *Technical Report Standards.* Sherman Oaks, CA: Banner Books International, 1977.

Keen, P. G. W. and M. S. Scott-Morton. *Decision Support Systems: An Organizational Perspective.* Reading, MA: Addison-Wesley, 1978.

Kelley, N. D. "Business Turns to Graphics." *Infosystems* 27 (November 1980): 51+.

Maier, M. *Basic Principles of Design.* New York: Van Nostrand Reinhold Company, 1977.

Marcus, A. "Computer-Assisted Chart Making From the Graphic Designer's Perspective." *Computer Graphics* 14 (July 1980): 247-253.

Myers, E. "Computer Graphics: Boom in Business Graphics." *Datamation* 27 (April 1981): 92-99.

Myers, W. "Computer Graphics: The Need for Graphics Design, Part One." *Computer* 14 (June 1981): 86-92.

Orr, J., ed. *The Complete Computer Graphics Management Anthology.* Chestnut Hill, MA: Management Roundtable, Fall 1981.

Paller, A. T. "Improving Management Productivity With Computer Graphics." *IEEE Computer Graphics and Applications* 1 (October 1981): 9-16.

Paller, A. T. et al. *Choosing the Right Chart.* San Diego, CA: Integrated Software Systems Corporation, 1981.

Schmid, C. F. and S. E. Schmid. *Handbook of Graphic Presentation.* Second edition. New York: John Wiley & Sons, 1979.

Sheridan, S. "Business Wakes Up to Color Graphics." *Optical Spectra* 15 (July 1981): 44-46.

Vindberg, A. "Designing a Good Graph." *Harvard Library of Computer Graphics*, Volume Seventeen. Cambridge, MA: Harvard University Laboratory for Computer Graphics & Spatial Analysis, 1981.

Vindberg, A. and J. George. "Computer Graphics and the Business Executive—The New Management Team." *IEEE Computer Graphics and Applications* 1 (January 1981): 57-71.

Zelazny, G. *Choosing & Using Charts*. New York: McKinsey & Company, Inc., 1972.

Color

Albers, J. *Interaction of Color*. New Haven: Yale University Press, 1975.

Billmeyer, F. and M. Saltzman. *Principles of Color Technology*. New York: Wiley-Interscience, 1980.

Birren, F., ed. *A Grammar of Color: Munsell*. New York: Van Nostrand Reinhold Company, 1969.

Birren, F., ed. *The Elements of Color*. A Treatise on the Color System of Johannes Itten Based on His Book The Art of Color. Translated by Ernst Van Hagen, New York: Van Nostrand Reinhold Company, 1970.

Boynton, R. *Human Color Vision*. New York: Holt, Rinehart & Winston, Inc., 1979.

Branley, F. M. *Color: From Rainbows to Lasers*. New York: Harper & Row Publishers, Inc., 1978.

Caddell, F. *Keys to Successful Color*. New York: Watson-Guptill, 1979.

Chamberlin, G. J. and D. G. Chamberlin. *Color: Its Measurement, Computation and Application*. Philadelphia: Heyden & Son, Inc., 1980.

D'Andrade, R. and M. Egan. "The Colors of Emotion." *American Ethnologist* Vol. 1 No. 1 (1974): 41-64.

Duff, D. J. "Color on Temperature Maps." *The Cartographic Journal* Vol. 10 No. 1 (1973): 17-21.

Evans, R. M. *The Perception of Color*. New York: John Wiley & Sons, 1974.

Friend, D. "Color Graphics Information Systems Boost Productivity." *Mini-Micro Systems* 13 (May 1980): 181-190.

Green, R. E. "Communicating With Color." *Audio-Visual Communications* 12 (November 1978): 14-18, 46-47.

Gruber, L. S. "Color Computer Graphics and Imaging with Polaroid 8x10 Polacolor Land Film and the Dunn 631 Color Camera." *Harvard Library of Computer Graphics*, Volume Nine. Cambridge, MA: Harvard University Laboratory for Computer Graphics & Spatial Analysis, 1980.

Hunt, R. W. G. *The Reproduction of Color*. Third edition. England: Fountain Press, 1975.

Hurvich, L. M. *Color Vision*. Sunderland, MA: Sinauer Assoc., 1981.

Itten, J. *The Art of Color*. The Subjective Experience and Objective Rationale of Color. Translated by Ernst Van Hagen. New York: Van Nostrand Reinhold Company, 1973.

Joblove, G. H. and D. P. Greenberg. "Color Spaces for Computer Graphics." *Computer Graphics* 12 (August 1978): 20-25.

Judd, D. B. and G. Wyszecki. *Color in Business, Science, and Industry*. Third edition. New York: John Wiley & Sons, 1975.

Kelly, K. L. and D. B. Judd. *Color: Universal Language and Dictionary of Names*. National Bureau of Standards Special Publication 440. Washington, DC: U.S. Department of Commerce, 1976.

Krebs, M. J. and J. D. Wolf. "Design Principles for the Use of Color in Displays." *Proceedings of the Society for Information Display* 20 (1st quarter 1979): 10-15.

Langridge, R. et al. "Real-Time Color Graphics in Studies of Molecular Interactions." *Science* 211 (February 13, 1981): 661-666.

Meyer, G. W. and D. P. Greenberg. "Perceptual Color Spaces for Computer Graphics." *Computer Graphics* 14 (July 1980): 254-261.

Montalvo, F. S. "Human Vision and Computer Graphics." *Computer Graphics* 13 (August 1979): 121-125.

Morris, J. G. "Using Color in Industrial Control Graphics." *Control Engineering* 26 (July 1979): 41-45.

Myers, W. "The Need for Graphics Design, Part Two." *Computer* 14 (July 1981): 82-88.

Pavey, D., ed. *Color*. Los Angeles, CA: The Knapp Press, 1980.

Priestly, J. *History and Present State of Discoveries Relating to Vision, Light and Colours*. Cohen, I. Bernard, ed. New York: Arno Press, 1981.

Shoup, R. "Color Table Animation." *Computer Graphics* 13 (August 1979): 8-13.

Smith, A. R. "Color Gamut Transform Pairs." *Computer Graphics* 12 (August 1978): 12-19.

Staff Report. "The Color Display." *Optical Spectra* (April 1980): 46-51.

Tanimoto, S. L. "Colormapping Techniques for Computer-aided Design and Verification of VLSI Systems." *Computers and Graphics* 5 (1980): 103-113.

Truckenbrod, J. "Effective Use of Color in Computer Graphics." *Computer Graphics* 15 (August 1981): 83-90.

Varley, H., ed. *Color*. An Architectural Digest Book. Los Angeles: The Knapp Press, 1980.

White, D. "Interactive Color Mapping." AUTO-CARTO IV. Proceedings of the International Symposium on Cartography and Computing: Applications in Health and Environment. Reston, VA: November 4-8, 1979.

Zakia, R. D. and H. N. Todd. *Color Primer 1 & 2*. New York: Morgan & Morgan, Inc., Publishers, 1974.

Technical Articles

Atherton, P., K. Weiler and D. Greenberg. "Polygon Shadow Generation." *Computer Graphics* 12 (August 1978): 275-281.

Baer, A., C. Eastman and M. Henrion. "A Survey of Geometric Modeling." Inst. Physical Planning Rep. 66. Pittsburgh: Carnegie-Mellon University, March 1977.

Blinn, J. F. "Computer Display of Curved Surfaces." Ph.D. dissertation, University of Utah, 1978.

Blinn, J. F. "Simulation of Wrinkled Surfaces." *Computer Graphics* 12 (August 1978): 286-292.

Blinn, J. F. and M. E. Newell. "Texture and Reflection in Computer Generated Images." *Communications of the ACM* 19 (October 1976): 542-547.

Catmull, E. "A Hidden-Surface Algorithm with Anti-Aliasing." *Computer Graphics* 12 (August 1978): 6-10.

Cook, R. L. and K. E. Torrance. "A Reflectance Model for Computer Graphics." *Computer Graphics* 15 (August 1981): 307-316.

Coons, S. A. "Surfaces for Computer Aided Design of Space Forms." Cambridge, MA: MIT Project MAC, Technical Report #41, June 1967.

Crow, F. C. "Shadow Algorithms for Computer Graphics." *Computer Graphics* 11 (Summer 1977): 242-248.

Feibush, E. A. and D. P. Greenberg. "Texture Rendering System for Architectural Design." *Computer Aided Design* 12 (March 1980): 67-71.

Feibush, E. A., A. M. Levoy and R. L. Cook. "Synthetic Texturing Using Digital Filters." *Computer Graphics* 14 (July 1980): 294-301.

Gouraud, H. "Computer Display of Curved Surfaces." Ph.D. dissertation, University of Utah, June 1971. Also, *IEEE Transactions on Computers* Vol. TC-20, June 1971.

Newell, M. E. "The Utilization of Procedure Models in Digital Image Synthesis." University of Utah Computer Science Dept., UTEC-CSc-76-218, Summer 1975.

Phong, B. T. "Illumination for Computer-generated Images." Ph.D. dissertation, University of Utah, July 1973. Also, *Communications of the ACM* 18 (June 1975): 311-317.

Picture System 2 User's Manual. Salt Lake City: Evans and Sutherland Computer Corp., 1976.

Robertz, W. and D. P. Greenberg, "A Graphical Input System for Computer-Aided Architectural Design." Fourth International Conference and Exhibition on Computers in Design Engineering. *CAD '80 Proceedings* 4 (March 1980): 715-723.

Sechrest, S. and D. P. Greenberg. "A Visible Polygon Reconstruction Algorithm." *Computer Graphics* 15 (August 1981).

Sutherland, I. E. *SKETCHPAD: A Man-Machine Graphical Communication System.* Cambridge, MA: MIT Lincoln Laboratory Technical Report #256, May 1965.

Sutherland, I., R. Sproull and R. Schumacker. "A Characterization of Ten Hidden Surface Algorithms." *ACM Computing Surveys* 6 (March 1974): 1-55.

Warnock, J. "A Hidden Surface Algorithm for Computer Generated Halftone Pictures." Computer Science Dept. C.S. Tech. Report 4-15, University of Utah, June 1969.

Watkins, G. S. "A Real-Time Visible Surface Algorithm." Ph.D. dissertation, University of Utah, June 1970.

Weiler, K. and P. Atherton. "Hidden Surface Removal Using Polygon Area Sorting." *Computer Graphics* 11 (Summer 1977).

Whitted, T. "An Improved Illumination Model for Shaded Display." *Communications of the ACM* 23 (June 1980): 343-349.

Index